Artificial Intelligence

An Essential Beginner's Guide to AI, Machine Learning, Robotics, The Internet of Things, Neural Networks, Deep Learning, Reinforcement Learning, and Our Future

Contents

Introduction

So, what is the deal with intelligent machines? Will they soon decide on things such as copyright infringement? How about self-driving trucks and cars? What kind of impact will smart machines have on society and the future of human jobs?

This book will give you a glimpse into the most fascinating topic of the 21st century—artificial intelligence (AI), a hypothetical simulation of a living brain inside a computer.

Some of the areas addressed in this book include:

- How the media's hunger for attention spreads AI myths

- How tech companies get more funding by claiming they use AI

- How scientists want to worship AI like a god and see themselves as priests

- The structure of the human brain and the urges that power it

- Big Data and how it impacts the possible creation of AI

- Theoretical methods of making a thinking computer

- The impact of seminal inventions on society

- Possible AI implementation, including use cases

    As it turns out, working AI that is as smart as a human is highly unlikely, and the three "sides" that have produced the most noise about AI have all done so for their selfish reasons. By compiling information and ideas from various sources, this e-book aims to show you how we are all being whipped into a consumer-oriented frenzy to shut down our conscious thinking processes.

So, what is actually going on? Read on and find out.

Chapter 1 – Confluence of Interests

What you are about to read defies all mainstream notions of artificial intelligence (AI) and challenges all the foregone conclusions regarding what intelligent machines actually are or can be. All of the most influential media, tech companies, and scientists harp on about AI, this majestic, mythical and multifaceted machine that will take away jobs ranging from a food server to a truck driver to a lawyer "tomorrow". However, scratching beneath the surface of these claims shows there is barely any truth to them and that there's a grand deception being played, but one that's not inherently malicious—it's all about the money.

The mainstream media has been starving for sales, views, and subscriptions to the point it now has to come out with bombastic claims that are simple enough for everyone to understand. What better claim than that of an AI, a concept so vague that it can do anything and everything? As the barrier to entry into the media market lowered, a random Swedish guy in a cubicle snorting into his microphone could get millions of views more than a mainstream news outlet. Radical times called for radical measures, such as announcing AI, driving fear-based sales, views, and subscriptions.

Companies claiming to involve AI in their products and services get more funding and extra attention from the mainstream media, which is in on the ploy. Want to make bricks? Announce you are making AI-designed bricks, and the media will do your marketing for you. Stage a flashy but ultimately misleading demonstration, and all the global media will give you attention.

Scientists want to feel respected, so what better way to become influential and admired than claiming there is an AI only they can access, understand, and interpret? If that sounds like priesthood, that is exactly what it is. Again, the more bombastic claims scientists can produce, the more funding they can get and more attention from the media.

These three groups fuel one another in an endless cycle of excitement and fear. When is the actual AI product coming out? Nobody actually wants to make one because it would reveal the ruse and show that the technology just isn't there yet. What we do have right now is a very simple smart machine that can crunch data, compare images, and make simple mechanical motions, such as lifting boxes. Everything else is just a myth that might not ever come true.

Chapter 2 – AI Myths

Your entire worldview with regards to AI has likely been molded by media, such as movies, books, and news articles. After all, the media are there to inform us about the world, but they also have a hidden agenda—to make money. Movies and books can keep to the author's message because they have several means of tie-in monetization, such as toys, cartoons, comics, and so on, but what about news articles? Newspapers auction off page space and hustle subscriptions, but websites peddling news almost exclusively rely on advertisements, meaning shoving ads at visitors, with each view earning a small fraction of a cent.

Not knowing how to create quality content and make money off of it, news websites that survive off of ad views have to create what is known as clickbait, instantly consumable articles with flashy headlines and little substance. Writers of such content are pushed to drive as much traffic to the website using any description that is not an outright lie, which often burns them out very quickly. There is entire machinery that produces clickbait on a steady basis, and once the curtain is lifted, you will never again enjoy 90% of "news" on the internet.

Web users appreciate neatly sorted information, making countdown lists a great clickbait method that provides a sense of anticipation that there is going to be a grand reveal at the end, which usually doesn't live up to expectations. For example, a clickbait headline could boast about "12 best rhubarb uses" or "7 worst shows on the TV". There could actually be useful, relevant information in those two articles, but the way their headlines are written suggests the hosting website doesn't care about providing value to readers but simply wants their clicks. Besides, calling something "top" or "worst" is highly subjective and tells less about the topic and more about the author, who is going to burn out and disappear quickly anyway.

Anything that arouses the most extreme of emotions, such as fear or anger, is a welcome addition to a clickbait headline. We don't have much control over those emotions since their evolutionary purpose was to keep us alive by commanding our attention; meeting a tiger in the wild will either make you want to run away or poke it with a sharp stick, but in both cases, you will be hyper-focused on the tiger. Hijacking this circuitry to grab the attention of visitors is best done using clickbait descriptors, such as "predator", "war", "deadly", "smash" and so on. This triggers the ancient survival hardware in visitors' brains and makes them glued to the website, coming back for another hit of fear and anger. Provoking disgust works too— since we are disgusted by things that would make us sick, such as foul smells that indicate rotten food and poisonous animals. Again, hyper-focus brain circuitry in action.

Riding popular trends is great for clickbait, so a headline could be using a celebrity name that is popular at a given moment to boost its traffic. Elon Musk was in nearly every clickbait headline in 2018, especially since he is an eccentric entrepreneur that shows little restraint. Using Donald Trump's name works too, as long as it's remotely true and doesn't open the website to lawsuits for outright lying. Movies, toys, urban legends—anything that's talked about by others is worth cramming into a headline as it increases the chances of the article scoring high in search engine results, which is a vaunted source of traffic for every clickbait website out there.

Uncertainty in the headline is another favorite clickbait method. Curiosity is an extremely strong survival urge that helped us find new sources of food, so a clickbait headline hijacking this part of our brain could state "you won't believe what happened next" or "you'd never imagine what he said next." Often enough, the article doesn't actually show what happened or was said next, but it doesn't matter because the website got your click and earned that blasted fraction of a cent. Questions in headlines have the same purpose and can almost always be answered by "no" without even reading the article or knowing anything about the topic.

Let's combine these four most common clickbait methods and make an article headline, such as "You won't believe these 12 deadly rhubarb uses by Elon Musk". It is a completely made-up headline, but it does arouse attention, doesn't it? Like a great movie, it takes the reader on a rollercoaster of emotion and simply commands clicks; whether the content justifies the click is another story entirely. Buzzfeed.com happens to be the undisputed "King of Clickbait".

What happens when these websites get hold of content related to AI? We get a mishmash of all the most exaggerated and incredulous details that are meant to simply make you click the headline but not actually understand the content so that tomorrow you will be coming back for more. Over time, and with tens of thousands of clickbait websites constantly churning out content, we get a writhing, seething mass of total nonsense that threatens to send internet denizens into a state of total panic. Boiled down and spread from one person to the next virally, this universe of nonsense becomes AI myths, which are easily repeatable, explainable yet unproven, unsourced, and perfectly enraging statements.

It is tempting to believe the production of AI myths is a coordinated action, but that would be giving the clickbait producers and internet denizens too much credit. Reality is much more layered than we expect and often has the prime causes of any given result obscured by time and anonymity of initial actors. Layered incompetence and greed are much more likely and observable causes of AI myths than some nebulous entity working from the shadows.

The human brain is a great tool, sharpened by constant use and adaptation but also one that, at times, becomes too efficient at doing certain things, turning passive and jumping to conclusions even when that turns out to be harmful. This reflex stemming from the limbic system helped a lot when it came to survival but today serves little purpose—except to fuel clickbait websites. The solution is always to take things with a small dose of skepticism until they are abundantly proven rather than taking them at face value.

Now let's take a look at some of the most popular AI myths and unravel them:

AI will be used in combat

Metro.co.uk brings us "World War 3 fears as Russia unveils army of murderous robots the size of horses"[1]. Note the keywords in the heading: "war", "fear", "army" and "murderous", all meant to provoke fear and anger, associating them with robots. There is a curious mention of horses, though the article doesn't explain why horses were chosen as a reference point; this is the enticing curiosity part of writing clickbait headlines as mentioned above.

As expected, article content doesn't live up to the headline and doesn't even link to the official demo[2]. It is a small tank where a soldier aiming his gun at a location also has the vehicle aimed at the same location, probably to provide flanking fire. The tank looks nothing like a horse but is armed with two grenade launchers and a

---

1   https://metro.co.uk/2019/03/25/world-war-3-fears-russia-unveils-army-murderous-robots-size-horses-9013726

2   https://www.youtube.com/watch?v=HfYuDHphx1M&feature=youtu.be

machine gun. Aerial drones flying in squads help spot targets behind cover.

Armies already have enough conventional weaponry to destroy the entire world several times over, though you probably won't take comfort in that fact. Nuclear weapons alone can wipe out every trace of life on Earth, save deep-water creatures, bacteria, and cockroaches, who can survive headless for weeks[3]. Fun fact: cockroaches don't actually have a brain, so one scientist decapitated them under a microscope and sealed the wound with wax; they survived due to nerve clumps throughout their body that replaced the lost head and let them react as if alive.

How did we deal with nuclear weapons? Almost all countries in the world got together in 1963 and signed the Partial Test Ban Treaty that is basically a pinky swear that they won't be testing nuclear weapons; those that still haven't signed include the Vatican, Mozambique, Zimbabwe, and Uzbekistan. Of course, this favors the United States the most—since they had already detonated nuclear weapons over 1,000 times in the Earth's atmosphere prior to the Treaty.

Chemical weapons give us another *12 gruesome ways to die you won't believe are true*. First used on an industrial scale in World War I, meaning over 100 years ago, chemicals such as mustard gas were indiscriminately sprayed from airplanes and lobbed using artillery, producing painful blisters, blindness, and lesions on lungs; those who survived often developed cancer. The result was that these chemicals were banned from use in warfare the same way nuclear weapons were.

If AI or robots become a threat to established world powers, rest assured they will be banned just like nuclear and chemical weapons. Anything that gives small countries a force multiplier, meaning a

---

3   https://www.scientificamerican.com/article/fact-or-fiction-cockroach-can-live-without-head/f

way to have one soldier do the damage of a hundred or more, will be swiftly locked away in a vault so nobody can use it against the world's superpowers. Also, note how in the article the robot is shown being used by the soldier, rather than gunning down targets on its own. That is because no army wants to have its weapons controlled by an AI that could develop a conscience and refuse to invade a country, shoot up civilians, or do enhanced interrogation to gather data.

The most stereotypical portrayal of wartime AI is in the movie *War Games*, where it crunches down a huge number of nuclear holocaust scenarios to realize that the only winning move is no move at all. It is a nice movie twist but also reveals a fatal weakness in AI, because why would any army use a machine that would recommend against all attacks or retaliations?

AI and smart machines can be given boring chores, such as digging trenches or carrying supplies back and forth. The problem is, what happens when the enemy inevitably captures one of our smart machines? How do we prevent all the resources and effort put into AI development simply being stolen by enemies and used against us? To that, there is no satisfying answer, which brings up interesting notions of reckless AI use backfiring against people who pushed it. This isn't inherent to just wartime use; even peacetime AI development will be liable to be easily stolen by the competitors through the internet.

Will AI be used in combat? Most likely not, as it is quite fragile and won't withstand the raw experience that makes grown men get PTSD. If robots do get used in warfare on a grand scale, we can expect all sides to use them equally, making war just another hyper-violent sport where nobody actually dies. If anything, AI will be used in disinformation campaigns to sow discontent online, which is a far more devastating use, but the headline of "You might have been reading AI's poor grammar without even knowing" just doesn't have the same clickbait appeal.

AI will take our jobs

This myth aims to stoke fears of losing job security, going straight for that part of the brain obsessed with survival. The notion of losing employment to an AI that vastly outperforms humans sounds plausible but also plays into and latches onto the fear of low-skilled immigrants taking all our jobs and being paid peanuts to do them; if a crummy immigrant can do it, why not a smart machine? Note this article headline "Self-driving vehicles are set to take 25,000 jobs a MONTH away from Americans with truck drivers being worst hit"[4]. Here we have the keywords "take", "worst", and "hit" in the headline. What is the catch?

The article authoritatively cites a Goldman Sachs report, which claims that in each year leading up to 2042 truck drivers will be losing jobs at a rate of up to 25,000 a month, with all four million trucking jobs gone by that year. A direct link to the report itself is conspicuously absent from the article, and there doesn't seem to be any trace of it online. Perhaps it was distributed through mail or other non-digital means, but let's just assume it does exist and those claims are valid. How does truck driving work now and how exactly are AI trucks supposed to "take away jobs"?

A truck driver is expected to haul cargo from point A to B in the shortest time possible using a truck supplied by the logistics company that hires anyone willing and able to do the task. The truck itself is usually in a state of advanced dilapidation, with maintenance cutting into the owner's company profit margins. Brakes are a particularly worrisome part, which led to plenty of US states implementing truck arrester beds[5], special lanes filled with coarse gravel where a truck with failed brakes can safely stop. Any trucker that stays in the business always has just one goal—buying his or her

---

4   https://www.dailymail.co.uk/sciencetech/article-4534752/Self-driving-cars-takeover-human-jobs.html

5   https://www.youtube.com/watch?v=_xqBZVnBkXl

own truck to have a reliable vehicle, making him or her an owner-operator, an independent contractor that can now bargain for better jobs from a favorable position.

Truck drivers are typically men with minimal education who can't find any other employment and rely on trucking as hard as possible to make quick cash—that is until the government decided to regulate the industry severely. Gone are the days where truckers were like cowboys, riding in a group, pushing rude drivers off the road and taking over empty stretches of desert highways to settle their scores, like in the 1978 movie *Convoy*[6]. To be fair, it was a lawless state of affairs, and it is hard to negotiate with a guy at the seat of a 40-ton truck who hasn't slept in six days, but there is regulation, and then there's overregulation.

Truck drivers now have to use mandatory log tracking devices, have trucks electronically limited to 65mph at most, take mandatory breaks, suffer obnoxious drivers, and have trouble finding parking space[7], causing plenty of them to quit. Churnover is a huge problem with truckers, but there is no shortage of cargo in need of hauling thanks to whiny consumers spoiled by Amazon's same-day delivery who will gladly leave a four-star review, which is a death sentence for any Amazon seller jostling for a perfect review score and a top spot in search results. When put like that, it is no wonder why AI trucks are so desperately needed—logistics companies need more workers than ever but can't find them to the point they are willing to use whatever they can get.

An AI truck would supposedly be able to skirt around all the mandatory work hours' regulation, though it too might need maintenance. This would best be done by a dedicated person riding inside the truck to take over when AI experiences issues, the truck fails mechanically, or someone tries to hijack the cargo. We can

---

6   https://www.youtube.com/watch?v=sA0OP_x_zLc

7   https://www.trucks.com/2017/08/15/truck-drivers-top-10-peeves/

even call that job "driving assistant specialist". The driving assistant specialist would need to have at least two replacements, so three persons for each AI truck, and have them take eight-hour shifts as the other two are resting in the back of the truck.

In essence, we now have to hire triple the workforce because of AI trucks, though the role of strictly being a driver isn't there anymore unless AI fails catastrophically. Would being a driving assistant specialist be a better or worse job than being a driver? That comes down to perspective, but one thing is for sure—it would pay a lot more because it would now require a more delicate skillset related to repairing and handling the AI truck. That sounds completely counterintuitive, but market trends have consistently shown that every new generation has been getting more chances for education and thus much better-paid jobs thanks to technology, not despite it.

Things will change with the advent of AI trucks, but it is productivity that matters, and those willing to put in skilled work will always have a way to earn an income, though it might not resemble the steady careers of yesteryear. No jobs will be "lost" because jobs aren't found in the first place, and no jobs will be "taken" because they don't exist in a limited quantity; they are created by market demand, and as the market grows so will the number of job opportunities for everyone, including AI trucks.

With advanced dilapidation, AI might cease to function as intended, at which point driving assistant specialists can take turns manually operating the truck, except that they are now legally covered for work hours' restrictions because technically the AI was driving. All market solutions for existing problems always loop back to the same old solutions because they work, and in the case of vehicles, it has to have a human on board; it is just that humans will now get paid more if they can learn how to handle an AI truck. By the way, every business imaginable scoffs at new technology, so unless the new solution flaunted in the media provides entrepreneurs with more legal maneuvering space or gives them more funding, just disregard it.

Stats on AI deployment in startups reveal the whole picture—the definition of AI is so muddled that around 40% out of 2,830 EU startups don't use any AI but brag about doing so as that gives them 15% more funding from investors[8]. Simply mention that your startup will be using "AI-reinforced machine learning supported by Big Data to make the world a better place"; it sounds great but means nothing, giving you a chance to get extra funding and media attention without added work or obligations.

Of course, the article mentions none of this context but simply slaps on a graph and calls it a day. A graph wouldn't lie to us, would it? You are not meant to understand the nuance of what is going on—simply give the website your click, absorb the underlying message of fear, and move on to the next headline. "Deadly rhubarb uses"—what the headline should be saying is, "If AI does get made and gets any traction, AI-driven trucks will open up more job opportunities for everyone" but optimism and measured portrayal of facts doesn't attract clicks fueled by fear and anger like clickbait does.

AI will be a romantic partner

This myth is particularly effective on women in their late 30s and early 40s who haven't started a family and are now wondering, "Where have all the good men gone?" Men are afflicted by a lack of intimacy too, but since they are by nature solitary and used to doing things on their own, they can survive with incidental physical relationships without having to form a steady connection. One Wired article titled "Falling in love with AI virtual assistants: a creepy love affair nearer than you think"[9] uses only one clickbait keyword—"creepy".

---

8   https://www.wired.co.uk/article/ai-venture-capital-startups

9   https://www.wired.co.uk/article/virtual-assistant-ai-love

The mainstay of the article is *Her*[10], a movie about a writer who feels lonely, buys an AI (s)assistant, and falls in love with her. Being able to share what he thinks and feels with someone, even if it is an AI, actually makes him happier and more productive at work because he finally feels there is someone out there who understands him. Now, a romantic connection is meant to be a prelude to sex, but in the movie, the topic is broached awkwardly and with a wholly unsatisfying conclusion. In the real world, we might be getting realistic sex dolls equipped with a barebones personality that might still be an attractive purchase for those who simply want to shake off that dreary feeling of loneliness.

Making an AI realistic enough will require it to become what is known as Turing complete, meaning indistinguishable from a human. The phrase stems from what was known as the "Turing test", a testing in which a human converses through text messages with another human and a computer in other rooms, with the assignment to distinguish which is which. "Turing complete" eventually came to be considered an inside joke in programming circles, as it implies an infinite test that evolves as we reach new scientific insights. But would a machine that consistently solved the Turing test even be enough?

Answering that question requires defining a perfect partner, which can be a touchy subject. What is an ideal relationship anyway? We can confidently conclude that a relationship where all parties can grow and help each other develop their full potential is the only sustainable one. So, will we be able to keep up with AI and will it be able to keep up with us? Probably not, as narrow AI will linger on as a highly-specialized chat partner and general AI will briefly appear human only to instantly evolve into super AI, an unnaturally smart machine that is way beyond our level. In all three cases, we are not likely to have AI fulfill our emotional, let alone sexual and intimacy, needs in the long run. We are simply not meant for each other.

---

10   https://www.imdb.com/title/tt1798709/?ref_=fn_al_tt_1

Actual relationships also involve conflicts that need to be resolved constructively to progress to the next level of emotional understanding. With AI, it is unlikely that there is going to be any such kind of conflict because it is going to be a product that's meant to boost customers' egos rather than provide an insurmountable challenge that requires psychological development. However, it will be a fun toy for a while, at least until AI is provided with human rights that prohibit foul language, domestic abuse, controlling behavior, and so on.

Chapter 3 – Manipulating the Limbic System

The way the human brain has been arranged by millions of years of evolution has centered on survival, which is why we can feel such strong fear and anger, both emotions that help us deal with danger. So, how is the human brain structured? Individual neurons are jammed together in a tough bone sheath and can network to exchange and reshape impulses from the outside world. How these neural pathways formed in childhood and how they communicate afterward is called "personality", a distinct set of preferences that we take great pride in, without even realizing how much of it is beyond our control or choosing.

At the basis of our brain is the limbic system that deals with core bodily functions, such as breathing and body temperature. That is the primal part of the brain that houses weird urges and phobias but also impulses, such as hunger, lust, and anxiety. The limbic system is encased in the neocortex, the part of the brain containing higher brain functions, such as logic and sense of humor. The limbic system helps us survive, but the neocortex helps us thrive, and the two are meant to cooperate but often have a distinct power dynamic.

The limbic system is so fast and powerful that it essentially gets to do what it wants in terms of the entire body and then we justify its actions with the neocortex, either by using logic to rationalize or humor to cope with what just happened. This autopilot functionality of our brain made sense in the African plains a million years ago, when a millisecond reaction at the moment of hearing grass rustle meant the difference between life and death. In today's society, the limbic system is largely hyperactive for no good reason, being constantly triggered by coordinated manipulation from the media, companies, and scientists who just want our attention.

Instead of activating only when our life is endangered, the limbic system is constantly bombarded by advertisements from businesses that realize all buying and consuming decisions stem from it. Sounds, sights, and smells all represent positive reinforcement meant to entice the limbic system's zones dealing with pleasure, addiction, and emotional experiences and create a customer for life. Companies are already exploiting these core, dormant behaviors that were once crucial for our survival to make money. However, there is more of these, and whoever can define them first will become unthinkably rich.

All marketing boils down to figuring out what forces lurk in the primal part of our brain and acting upon them directly to override conscious thoughts. Marketing AI will be no different, and you can already see how it is being touted as the perfect tool to wage war, do murder, end hunger and loneliness, all of which aim directly at the limbic system. Computer programmers also have to deal with the limbic system, mainly by using what is known as UX or user experience, which is trying to figure out where the user will experience irrational anger, pleasure or anguish during the use of an interface.

What is interesting is that there's a number of parallels between the brain and computer structure. The limbic system corresponds to a kernel, a core component in computers, while the neocortex is just like the operating system. So, as soon as you press the power button on your computer, the kernel starts up and coordinates everything else, bootstrapping the operating system that you can work with; the kernel itself is inaccessible and thus shielded from tampering. An average computer user has no clue that there is such a thing as a kernel or what it does because the clicky-clicky desktop environment works just fine.

Arguably, there is a reason why computers are structured like the human brain—it is the most perfect tool in existence. We are using the brain for menial tasks without even knowing how it works or why, which is the same as an average person just playing Solitaire on his or her desktop computer. It is no wonder AI is expected to arise from a digital arrangement that looks like the human brain; what else could we possibly use?

The implication is that AI will be using a digital replica of the human brain, skipping over a couple of million years of evolution in a jiffy to teach us about how our brain works and where we should be looking next. Since it won't have to struggle for survival, this would imply AI won't have the limbic system, allowing it to think in perfect clarity and without survival impulses that cloud our judgment, giving us scientific and psychological breakthroughs our puny brains can't even comprehend.

These are just some of the fascinating behaviors burrowed deep in our brains that are being acted upon daily by the environment. There is much reputable academic literature on the limbic system, but it is all so unbearably dry and soporific—seeing it play out right in front of your eyes is quite different, isn't it? What is most notable is that it's extremely hard to stop these urges, but that can be done if we only use our free will, roughly defined as "awareness of choices".

Every religion and educational system is meant to tell us that we don't have to obey our urges, or at least that is what they were initially designed for; over time, all systems that support the neocortex crumble and start affecting the limbic system as it is much faster and compliant. This erodes our free will because it strengthens our primal urges, inevitably leading us to complacency and ruin. Understanding how the human brain works and how it is being manipulated daily is essential to maturity and psychological development. The thing is, thanks to the internet, we now have more sources of information and wisdom than ever before, allowing us to all share and grow together.

Chapter 4 – Motivation for Creating AI

The idea of having a brainless, unthinking, unfeeling but completely obedient automaton at our command has been fascinating humans for millennia. Jewish folklore gave us the golem, a creature made out of mud or clay and animated by inscribing a magical word on its forehead. This act mimicked the very creation of Adam by God, as described in Genesis 2:7[11]: "Then the Lord God formed a man from the dust of the ground and breathed into his nostrils the breath of life, and the man became a living being." This is also why burial rites in Christians include the words "dust to dust", that being a reminder that the ineffable Divine is what gave us our life but we ultimately have to admit subordination and subservience to the natural order of things. We can create life but can't endow inanimate objects with it.

This concept of making a golem, taking inanimate matter and giving it life, thus encapsulates the notions of challenging God himself, becoming creators of life, finding a shortcut to maturity, lust for

---

11
       https://www.biblegateway.com/passage/?search=Genesis+2%3A7&versio
n=NIV

power, pride, and desire to stave off death, the inevitable return to the dust from which we all came. There is a good reason stories such as those involving golems have survived in our collective consciousness—they show us the underlying, background thought processes running in our minds and constantly affecting our daily lives, just like it would happen on a computer.

We all want to have more power, whether that means more energy, more muscles, or just more control over how specific things pan out. The reason for this is that our ancestors who craved power were usually the ones to get it and continue the lineage; those who were meek got swept aside by natural forces and died out. The genetic code we carry is a compilation of behaviors that led to the survival and procreation of our ancestors, and so our genes force us to do the same. It is a completely involuntary drive that we can try to curb up to a point, but we will have to yield sooner or later. So, we'll want to create a golem of some sort, though we might call it a different name and attach fanciful explanations to the act to appease the rational part of the mind, but the raw truth is that we want more power to survive.

Just a quick note: if Adam was a golem created by God, how did that story turn out? Spoilers—God gives Adam a highly specific command, Adam disobeys and is thus disowned and cast out of paradise by his creator. The snake that prompted the tasting of the forbidden fruit can be said to represent a small, unexpected variable or influence, such as a computer virus or a bug. Whoever wrote the Genesis story shrewdly noticed that there are behavior patterns that seem to be repeating themselves with or without technology and left a reminder to all future generations, admittedly shrouded as religious teaching. By the looks of it, we will go through the same Genesis story with AI as we try to make an obedient servant that is supposed to empower us but will inadvertently betray us due to some random corrupting influence.

To be fair, it is not our fault—the brain we are using is both the most modern biological machine and the most outdated one at the same time. We're capable of absorbing untold amounts of information and connecting it in completely novel ways, but we're also running these outdated survival instructions that originate from the caveman era and can override every other thought.

For example, our brain is telling us to eat all the food in our vicinity because cavemen who gorged on food survived through scarcity; the problem is that we are on average living in such caloric abundance that obesity is a huge health risk, but we still crave food. It is like using a computer that hasn't been updated in 20,000 years that constantly launches an application we have to keep shutting down just to do the most basic daily tasks.

Human behavior is what is known as emergent property, a spontaneous appearance of a heretofore unknown function. We have very little idea of how and why human behavior appears, but we can speculate. The brain is made up of neurons, which are highly conductive bioelectrical components wrapped in layers of fat that serve as insulation. On their own, neurons can't do much of anything, but when billions of them are crammed together inside a skull, fed, kept cozy, and allowed to network, they can produce the human consciousness, culture, and self-awareness. There is a good reason why we say "brain surgery" for anything excessively complex; we use the brain daily but know very little about how it works, why it fails, and how to fix it.

How does this relate to AI? Well, machine learning is about giving digital devices the adaptability of a living brain or, to be more specific, of a single neuron that can process individual bits of data and provide some utility to the owner. When these digital neurons are strung together in massive arrays, they exponentially increase each other's processing power in a way living neurons do. Since we now possess an environment peppered with tiny IoT devices, each of which can process individual bits of data to provide some utility to the owner, we might get a monumental digital brain the size of a continent and a spontaneously emerging AI. What other emergent properties will this kind of digital brain develop? We don't know, which is for scientists the best possible introduction to "let's find out".

What we do know is that other living beings can organize themselves in intelligent ways to make up for their lack of individual strength. Volvox is a species of freshwater algae that form colonies of up to 50,000 units. Each of them is a separate cell and may survive on its own, but together they move, feed, and reproduce in unison. With hardened cells on the outskirts, primitive eyes that can sense light, and tiny tentacles serving as oars that move the entire colony towards the light, i.e., the power source, Volvox is an example of how a group of simple organisms can work together to create something bigger and more prosperous.

Why do algae band together? They don't have any capability for reasoning or abstract planning but somehow appear to sense power in one another and understand their chance of survival is much higher if they cooperate. We know that lions and hyenas hunt in packs to increase their chances of taking down big game, while birds migrate in massive flocks to easily cut through wind resistance and allow the weakest members to coast along.

Chapter 5 – Basic Concepts

The concept of machines that can evolve by learning from the environment has been discussed in the scientific community for nearly a century. As with all advanced paradigms, machine learning was first mocked, then considered, and then wholeheartedly embraced. The problem with machine learning is that computers don't have a filtering mechanism to sort out information like living brains do, and they can't create organizations of higher order like humans. We can quickly assess if something is unworthy of our attention to save our energy for actual tasks under the guidance of a smarter, more efficient person, but computers can't handle the actual world in either way. Smart machines are thus fed filtered data arranged in sets, with their learning environment being kept completely sterile, so to speak.

Exposing smart machines to the outside world usually ends in disaster as their frail brains become clogged with useless information. For example, there is a smart machine watching what you type into Google Search, and by being hooked into your personal profile assembled courtesy of Gmail, YouTube, and other Google services, can recommend personalized search results. You are not meant to know about this smart machine because you might want to feed it false information, corrupting the results it provides. If enough users did this, Google Search would essentially be rendered worthless.

The structure of a smart computer is like the Congress in that it is made out of small, independent units that can vote on any given thing. When additional layers are built on top of this arrangement, we can think of it as creating the Senate, which can also add input on matters. Think about the prolonged political discussions that eventually have to boil down to a Yay or Nay vote; that is essentially how a smart machine works. Note that a smart machine takes in binary data but outputs probability, meaning it can be more or less certain about the result and thus we can rate any neural network's quality by estimating how correctly it guessed what we wanted it to do, but it is never *certain*.

With enough layers, we can start talking about a neural network, where different layers have different weights attached to them depending on their performance. In short, the neural network can differentiate between units and their votes depending on how they performed in the past. Think of it as driving to work and barely listening to a voice on the radio but then giving your full attention to your boss at work; the neural network *learns to ration* its computational resources. At this point, machine learning becomes deep learning, where the neural network reorganizes itself according to its own principles that we don't fully understand at speeds we can't keep track of.

Feeding the neural network consistent datasets and showing it what we want the result to be is called "reinforcement learning" and produces a highly-specialized smart machine. For example, showing images of dogs or cats will reinforce the concepts of "dog" or "cat", but showing both will make the neural network much better at recognizing animals in general. Depending on what the intended use of the neural network is, scientists train it differently using data gathered from publicly available sources.

When a neural network is attached to a specific piece of hardware, we can start talking about robotics, which is essentially giving a neural network a body. The robot can have different levels of mobility or just be stationary, like Alexa's speaker that is meant to be put on the table and listen to occupants. Some advances have been made in letting the neural network decide where and how it wants to move in the world, but again, it is all workable while it's in a safe, controlled environment; any interference by humans or animals usually wrecks the robot. When there are so many robots around us that they form their own neural network, but with hardware instead of software units, is when we can start talking about the internet of things (IoT).

Chapter 6 – IoT Ecosystem

Our businesses scale, but our ways of doing business don't, which is why we have this push for automation and adoption of artificially intelligent systems. Countries and companies that adopt IoT will gain the upper hand, forcing everyone else to do the same. This opens companies and governments to hacking attacks thanks to the concept of the attack surface, wherein the more systems are networked together, the lower their overall security as a remote attacker can breach the weakest link to breach the entire network.

The main advantage of IoT, as touted by producers of various robots it consists of, is being able to quickly make tiny decisions based off of data gathered through sensors or fed to it from some external source. For example, Roomba sweeps the floor while relying on its sensors to relieve you of having to stand by with a dustpan. Sounds good but the main disadvantage of Roomba is that it relies on regular maintenance, so now you are standing by with a screwdriver instead of a dustpan. What if we made a second Roomba that fixed the first one and let them work in tandem?

We would obviously need a third Roomba with the ability to diagnose malfunctions, capable of overseeing the first one's sweeping to detect when and why it broke and to send out the second one. The three Roombas would already be an IoT ecosystem that could work on its own without having to wait for sluggish humans' input. If the three Roombas had to cover a huge area and communicated through a wireless connection, now we could employ a fourth Roomba working as a mobile router that would follow the trio around and position itself for maximum network performance.

The problem then becomes that computer systems typically experience an exponential increase in attack surface with a linear increase in complexity. Anyone in the vicinity with the know-how to make and use an antenna could hack into our Roomba quartet and do with it as he pleases. So, now we could employ 55 Roombas with machine guns that gunned down everyone coming, but that wouldn't solve the inherent weakness in the concept that undercuts any utility such an ecosystem might have. However, if our Roombas are in a closed system, such as a warehouse, that same weakness is largely eliminated.

By eliminating human interference, an IoT ecosystem allows robots to cooperate at speeds, coordination, and endurance well beyond what humans are capable of. Any humans present on the location would typically be just passive observers, without even having the ability to manually override the robots, which has so far happened with Google's Waymo, a self-driving shuttle car that has no steering wheel or brakes. Tech giants envision the future in which homes, schools, and hospitals become the same kind of sterile environment for the AI, with humans showing ultimate respect and obedience. For now, Amazon is the one to be making that vision closest to reality.

Amazon warehouses, also called "fulfillment centers", are places where an IoT ecosystem is already enhancing the human workforce and might soon be replacing it; humans still pick items, sort and pack them, but those work positions are likely to become automated too, thanks to robots such as Boston Dynamics' Handle[12], an ostrich-like robot that can move boxes on its own.

Boasting a hard work tempo and strict conditions that tolerate no tardiness[13], these gigantic warehouses host robots that cart massive quantities of items by gliding along the special concrete floor and reading QR codes to navigate to their destination. Rollers and conveyor belts shuttle items left and right and it is all due to wanting to deliver that gift or order as soon as possible. The end goal is to have Amazon selling all products in the world to every customer at once; Amazon is actually losing billions of dollars on sales because it's focused on growth, not making a profit.

---

12   https://www.youtube.com/watch?v=5iV_hB08Uns

13   https://www.wired.com/2014/06/inside-amazon-warehouse/

Chapter 7 – Fighting Against Tech Giants

With the advent of the internet, we now have at our disposal digital tools and methods to propagate information, which is what an AI uses to feed itself. A local economy could afford to adopt something like the steam engine at its own pace, but the emergence of AI will mandate that we restrict access to information and curb the growth of tech companies that recklessly seed our environment with uncontrollably growing services, which is what the European Union (EU) is already doing.

The EU is fighting back against US tech giants, most notably by introducing sweeping legal frameworks intended to curb their influence in the EU market. As explained in one CNN article[14], EU is dead set on breaking Google apart through fines and regulatory action. In March 2019, EU voted in a copyright directive[15] that contains the now-infamous Article 11 and Article 13, which

---

14   https://edition.cnn.com/2019/03/20/tech/eu-antitrust-google/index.html

15   https://eur-lex.europa.eu/legal-content/EN/TXT/?uri=CELEX%3A52016PC0593

respectively mandate a news aggregator service to ask for permission or pay a license fee before linking to a news article and that content providers have to respect copyright at all times, not just when big companies ask them to. In short, Article 11 and 13 all but explicitly name Google News and YouTube, both of which attach ads to someone's content and make money by the truckload while paying a pittance to select content creators.

How is Google supposed to scan hundreds of thousands of hours of video being uploaded round the clock to YouTube for copyright infringement? While Google does possess ContentID, a system for checking uploaded content against an established database of work belonging to major publishers, there is very little that can be done to apply ContentID before the video is uploaded, which is what Google would have to start doing. The main problem is that YouTube has grown way beyond what any company can handle, and it was perfectly on purpose by Google.

YouTube was meant to be a massive siphon for information, the most comprehensive dataset in video form for training an AI in object recognition and trend analysis. YouTube videos also make money by having ads shown next to them, allowing Google to just keep expanding the infrastructure and pocket the difference without having to create any content at all. By the time you are reading this, it is likely that YouTube is not the same anymore, becoming fragmented or restricted for most users, which the EU regulators expected and planned for. Google won't abate its data collection efforts and is likely to simply shift to some other data source, such as IoT gadgets. We all have smartphones, which can easily have Google apps baked into them, for which the EU has actually punished Google as it promoted a monopoly. But when it comes to YouTube, it is all about the tricky business of copyright.

Legally, copyright owners have absolute rights to their content and can even pass them on to their progeny or sell them to any company. A copyright owner can rent or sell any part of his or her content while placing any restrictions imaginable on it for free or at a price.

However, content gets remixed by the general public all the time, which makes copyright void since it only concerns exact copies, but that is determined through a lengthy and costly court process the copyright owner is all but guaranteed to win. The problem is that changing just 0.01% of copyrighted content doesn't provide the same legal protection as changing 99.99% of it; copyright covers the exact expression of ideas but not ideas themselves.

When Google got hold of YouTube and users started uploading enormous quantities of content, huge copyright owners, such as Warner Brothers, started rubbing their hands; Google was serving ads alongside the content, becoming liable for copyright infringement since it was making money off of copyrighted content. Solution? Create an automated system that reviews all uploaded videos and compares them to the copyrighted content database created by big companies that are eager to sue Google into oblivion if infringements continue.

This ContentID flagging system has been shown as a spectacular failure, correctly recognizing copyrighted content only for as long as exact copies of big-brand content were uploaded. Once small content producers started recording and copyrighting noise, such as wind chimes, entire swaths of YouTube content got flagged for copyright infringement. In 2015, ContentID issued a copyright strike against a video that contained nothing else but a purring cat[16], claiming the sound belonged to EMI Music Publishing. Technically, cat owner could sue Google and EMI for false copyright claims, but that is again another costly court process that nobody is willing to undergo, so things get settled by Google defaulting towards whatever benefits copyright holders.

Scaled up, ContentID simply doesn't work because it is tilted towards shielding Google from lawsuits, not making sure copyright owners or YouTube users get their needs met. There simply needs to

---

16   https://torrentfreak.com/youtube-flags-cat-purring-as-copyright-infringing-music-150211/

be a human at the helm reviewing copyright claims and either approving or dismissing them; there is no conceivable way AI can ever take this duty over. YouTube alone has something like 3,000 hours of video uploaded every second, with no kind of support staff to review it all for copyright infringement and community guidelines adherence; it is relegated to the hive-mind intelligence, whether it's humans or machines.

Google tried introducing a model of YouTube Heroes as a way to incentivize users to essentially become unpaid content reviewers, which is, in theory, a good idea, but was mercilessly panned by all YouTube content creators as being tyrannical and exploitative. If Google had AI or anything close to it ready for deployment, it would have been deployed already on YouTube; if ContentID is the vaunted AI, we can see it is a disaster. This is only copyright claims, a nebulous right that AI is woefully inadequate in handling, yet we are supposed to think that AI is market-ready and coming to take our jobs.

Neural networks inhabiting IoT devices and phoning back home to report on the real world and actions of humans in it can be said to represent AI sensory organs. These tiny robotic units can feed massive quantities of real-time data to the AI, letting it simulate reality and attempt to predict future trends. We all impact one another and the tiniest of our actions have long-reaching consequences that we typically ignore, but an AI that has insight into all the IoT device data feeds in a tightly controlled environment devoid of free will would be able to be omnipresent and omniscient.

Here is where we embark on a strange journey into deep subconscious thoughts of humans, especially those related to obedience towards a higher status person. If a command is given by another human, we assess his or her status relative to ours and comply if it is higher; a deity is automatically afforded ultimate respect and presumed infallible. Therefore, if a tech giant wanted to push total acceptance of IoT and the intrusion of privacy that involves, the best way would be to present an AI crunching all the data feeds from hardware as a godlike entity. That doesn't mean any of it would be actually true but simply that the owner company would market it that way to achieve total market penetration and exclude the competition under a literal accusation of heresy.

The idea is that this kind of AI would be welcomed with open arms, as it could properly arrange every little thing we are doing in our daily life to make it better, provided we don't interfere with it in any way. From finding perfect employment to predicting future crime and being the perfect partner for everyone, such an AI would, in theory, be able to run an entire metropolis like clockwork, fixing problems before they appear. Note that this is still science fiction, but every tech giant that wants more IoT devices in the open to gain more data feeds will sooner or later tout this kind of arrangement as inevitable and positive, with AI serving the role of a benevolent god. For some people, this is already the case.

George Hotz is a true believer in AI and its ability to transform the future, despite already having a successful self-driving car venture and knowing the inherent limitations of AI—namely that it is probabilistic rather than deterministic. Pay attention to how closely what he is saying in a 2019 article from The Verge titled "Comma.ai founder George Hotz wants to free humanity from the AI simulation"[17] matches a religious sermon. At the annual SXSW tech conference held in Austin, Texas, George held a speech about the idea that we are all living in a simulated universe and that breaking out of it would let us meet God and kill him.

George's sermon is supported by mainstream musings of scientists who say we might all be just characters in a video game made by an extremely advanced intelligence. The same way we create and engage in scenarios where characters follow our rules and exist within the framework we give them, but only have "life" when we are micromanaging them, we might be someone's entertainment,

---

17   https://www.theverge.com/2019/3/9/18258030/george-hotz-ai-simulation-jailbreaking-reality-sxsw-2019

except that we also have a degree of free will to make things interesting.

According to a Scientific American article[18] that quotes Neil deGrasse Tyson, there is a 50-50 chance our entire universe is just a simulation on someone's cosmic hard drive. After noting that our DNA differs from chimpanzees by only 2%, Neil said that there could be such a form of intelligence that would make us look as primitive as chimps; that same intelligence would be entertaining itself with creating and editing the human race.

The simulation theory stems from Nick Bostrum, who in 2003 suggested our super advanced progeny could one day decide to run a simulation of ancestors—us—on their mega computers. Our lives right now could be just a flicker of an imaginary dream, and we wouldn't be able to tell whether any other person is a simulation of a real mind or just a side character in this massive charade.

Simulation theory is corroborated by the fact that all natural laws in our universe seem to be mathematically correlated, just like if a conscious mind made them. Other scientists lamented the fact that such an improbable hypothesis was considered at all, claiming the likelihood of the simulation theory is effectively zero. How does one even begin to test the simulation theory?

It gets worse. The simulation theory also states that we might be living in a computer game, with game designers cutting corners to save on their computational resources, which is meant to explain paranormal phenomena, such as ghosts, clairvoyance and deja vu. There are even MIT physicists, such as Zohreh Davoudi, who chip in with their musings on the topic, stating that since we have limited resources for running computer simulations so would our own godlike creators. Another interesting idea is that measuring cosmic rays shows they aren't continuous but have breaking points, like if

---

18   https://www.scientificamerican.com/article/are-we-living-in-a-computer-simulation/

we zoomed in on a picture and saw pixels that told us it is a file and not the real thing.

Philosophers are welcome to jump in the fray, which they do, stating that any evidence that we are in a simulation could also be a part of the simulation. Death would then be creators terminating those parts of the simulation that haven't produced anything interesting, so the advice for immortality would be "go do fun stuff". This also raises awkward questions about the soul, immortality, and reincarnation, which turns any scientific discussion sour. It is funny to consider that religious texts scientists consider backward and outdated might be the most advanced form of science because it all comes back to the human experience.

What would God be replaced by? You probably know the answer already—AI. George compares programming to magic, mentions humans likely have no free will, and belabors starting a religion focused on breaking out of the simulation. According to George, capitalism is spent as all companies inevitably set themselves up for failure by looking to maximize profits at all costs; a corporation should closely resemble a church to succeed in the long run. The turning point in our history will be what is known in the tech industry as "singularity", a point where the disconnected units in the IoT ecosystem gain critical mass and turn from disjointed robotic hardware doohickeys into living entities representing the super AI, a godlike emergent property of a neural network.

While singularity has been envisioned before, prominent exponents of it, such as Ray Kurzweil, primarily focused on implanting the technology in our bodies, but George Hotz talks about implanting the idea in our minds. We should forget about bettering ourselves or making money to gain more creature comforts and simply yield to the super AI and start having faith in this ultimate New Age religion. In both Ray's and George's version of singularity, capitalism is an outdated mode of thinking we should get past to become a part of the collective, representing the ultimate socialist Utopia where cash flows freely, and we can live without having to work.

Despite generating more wealth than any other form of societal organization in history and distributing it further than ever before, capitalism has been maligned by certain ideologies related to socialism as evil incarnate. Since AI will boost capitalism sky-high, tech giants might want to represent it as being godlike without actually being such to overcome this skepticism and resistance. Some pittance could also be distributed to the unwashed masses who adopt AI through universal basic income (UBI), again to sate socialist revolutionaries.

The late Stephen Hawking, Elon Musk, and Mark Zuckerberg have all at some point referred to the idea of UBI as necessary for when AI inevitably leaves humans jobless. As stated previously, that is highly unlikely to happen as it's humans who can create job openings faster than they can create and adopt AI that can fill them. One article[19] on Medium.com notes that installing AI into society will cause it comprehensive trauma and UBI will serve to cushion citizens from the economic crisis, stating that a 2020 US presidential candidate, Andrew Yang, already offered to introduce UBI. Both Republicans and Democrats actually agree on UBI; the former could see it happen without any new taxes while the latter would enjoy bragging about increased social benefits for minorities.

Mark Cuban opposes UBI, calling it "the worst possible response" to joblessness[20]. AI Superpowers blog, which sells the eponymous book[21] written by Dr. Kai-Fu Lee, argues that governments should provide minimum basic services (healthcare, food, shelter, and education) to citizenry for free, and then cash to those people involved with helping provide minimum basic services to others who

---

19   https://medium.com/datadriveninvestor/senseless-leisure-ubi-and-artificial-intelligence-3ff0312eed93

20   https://www.cnbc.com/2017/02/22/mark-cuban-basic-income-worst-response-to-job-losses-from-robots-ai.html

21   https://aisuperpowers.com/ai-and-you/ai-and-your-government

don't want to get involved. In essence, only government/AI employees would be getting UBI as a form of salary.

How would UBI differ from current welfare? The hidden claim behind UBI is that it is possible to find such an amount of cash that is adequate for everyone but looking at how real life plays out shows that is not the case. Young, single men are much more self-sustainable than most other categories, while categories like single moms require extra cash to deal with the burden of having a child raised by the state. How about disability or chronic health conditions, such as diabetes and mental illness? If we start considering age, sex, marital status, and overall health, all of a sudden, our UBI turns from being a simple, neat concept explainable in a few words to an administrative mess that goes back to being just the same kind of welfare we are already using within a few decades.

Without welfare, the tribal instinct kicks in, and people start organizing themselves into loosely affiliated clans that inevitably want to displace one another and gobble up the resources, leading to balkanization. It is another one of those pesky instincts coming from the limbic system, and we have done so much to appease it, but where do we go from here?

The romantic notion of replacing capitalism with some other form of governance more closely aligned with religion will ultimately be aimed at the lowest rungs of society, those who consider entrepreneurs and capitalists thoroughly evil and morally corrupt due to their desire to succeed. Everyone else can perceive the tremendous amount of wealth and productivity brought about by capitalism, wanting to participate and contribute to the economic growth willingly, but these discontents won't be so easily appeased with just wealth; they'll need something better.

What is likely to happen is that technology will have more and more separate haves and have-nots, leading to widespread resentment coming from those who can't relinquish outdated ideas or reconcile themselves with merit-based competency hierarchies. Those who can afford the latest iPhone or get involved in the IoT ecosystem will get all the benefits of AI that entails, while outsiders become a well of frustration, dragging everyone down and possibly causing riots that would make the elite huddle in their ultra-safe city fortresses turned into bunkers.

Growing societal tension and strife would then be rectified by tech giants presenting AI as a universal combination of religion and capitalism, touted as a necessary part of our lives. If a tech giant strikes a deal with the medical and pharmaceutical industry, the faithful can be equipped with IoT hardware that will create additional medical data sources for the company while drip-feeding users with drugs and vaccines. Therefore, the perfect business plan for marketing AI is revealed:

• present AI as a way to settle societal differences and make everyone equal, just like Facebook is already doing. To those who believe in capitalist ideas, AI should be presented as a way to increase productivity and personal wealth; to those who believe in religious concepts, AI should be presented as a benevolent "guardian angel" that's in accordance with their religious teachings. Concept of AI can be spun every which way to align with the ideals of all subcultures in the society the same way Facebook is a news source for some and a source of entertainment for others.

• use IoT devices that constantly scan the environment and gather data to report everything back to the mothership regardless of what the user wants, which is what Alexa is already doing. Shamelessly invade everyone's privacy through outright surveillance and create a detailed, thorough privacy policy that explains nothing and is buried deep within pages of legalese. This will create data feeds to help the company analyze user trends and sell off data to advertisers while minimizing legal liability. Any responsibility for the intrusion of privacy should always be placed on the user.

• medical devices have to undergo extensive clinical testing, but medical wearables don't (see Apple Watch that's being sold as a watch while being a fully functional medical wearable). Therefore, the IoT hardware should be sold in the form of a ring, bracelet, or necklace under the guise of jewelry or an accessory while claiming to provide some intangible medical benefit to the wearer. Certain body implants are also excluded from clinical testing, such as earrings and nose piercings, so one potential avenue of revenue would be creating IoT versions of such jewelry that could be installed in outpatient procedures or tattoo parlors.

• pharmaceutical companies typically have ironclad monopolies on the market, allowing them to deny competition from bringing down the prices of medication. Striking a deal with one such cartel may be coupled with giving IoT medical wearables the capability of injecting the wearer with a drug needed to control a chronic condition, preferably insulin to treat diabetes. Being mostly a lifestyle illness, diabetes disproportionately strikes minorities, which would allow the company to present itself as socially conscious, hide from negative publicity by claiming to "just want to help", and reap tremendous revenue from programs intended to help minorities battle chronic conditions, primarily Obamacare.

• IoT medical wearables should be designed based off of lessons learned from social networks to create a psychological addiction in users. Facebook, Instagram, and other social media notably use visual and audio cues to trigger a short-lived burst of satisfaction and remind the user to stay focused. In the case of medical wearables, the goal would be to remind the user to keep the wearable on lest their peers shame them for not being able to receive the latest notification or another such reward cue. The IoT medical wearable should be presented as a status symbol and being "cool" or even award meaningless points for being worn, which could eventually include the social credit system (SCS).

• minimize all expenses related to security and safety, the same way CloudPets has done by storing the recording of kids' messages on an unsecured Amazon cloud. Where possible, use the cheapest materials, freelance programmers, and open source software to cut down on development expenses. This will also lead to medical wearables quickly being damaged and outdated, necessitating another purchase by the user. When inevitable hacking attacks and security issues occur, spin the event as inconsequential and accuse whoever revealed the problem as being a Luddite and a rabble-rouser.

- vaccines give resistance but not immunity to disease and represent medicine that can be infinitely sold to a healthy person monthly or yearly. Pharmaceutical companies have near total immunity from lawsuits when it comes to vaccines, meaning they can fail without the customer having any legal recourse. In case that happens, the pharmaceutical company can earn extra profit by selling the medication for the disease its vaccine was meant to prevent.

All of this is possible thanks to "minimum viable product", the concept of producing just what makes the company legally shielded from false advertising lawsuits. This is a fairly common concept that exploits impulsive purchases, availability of funds in the Western world, and overall apathy of consumers when it comes to researching products and services before spending money on them. To be fair, customers can organize a class action lawsuit to recover damages, but the idea is to make as much money as possible before that and then weather the consequences. Any complaints about lacking functionality can be easily deflected by simply producing another model of the same product that is marginally better or offering a premium version at a much higher price.

As you can clearly see, the US market is ripe for the taking by anyone who wants to invest a little bit of time and effort in creating just the perfect kind of AI product to strike all the right chords. Racial tension, burgeoning healthcare costs, growing wealth divide, pharmaceutical monopolies, and centralization of power in megacities are already happening, so why not profit off of them while taking total control of the market? The AI doesn't even have to exist at the backend of this IoT medical wearable, but as long as users think there is or at least they aren't explicitly told there isn't, it is all kosher. Passing off AI as a religion might even qualify the tech company for some legal protections, most notably those related to religious freedom of speech and taxation.

The reason why these shenanigans are allowed is that US legislators figured out they can use US-based companies as an extension of military force to conquer the world economically. Why invade China if the Chinese adore iPhones and keep buying them, sending money to the US while letting a US-based AI analyze their private data? On the other hand, China might attempt something similar with Chinese hardware, most notably routers. Speaking of which, do you know who made your internet router? In all likelihood, it was a Chinese company who might have installed a backdoor, hidden access point for those in the know.

Militarily, the world is in a stalemate, which made superpowers organize blocs that vie for economic supremacy. The EU is one, as are the two Americas. China and Russia are eyeing India and Africa while poor Australia is left to fend for itself. Whoever reaches general AI first will be rocket-boosted into the new Golden Age of prosperity, with everyone else lagging behind. For now, each bloc has different strengths and leverages them differently in this global game of Monopoly.

Rare earth minerals are what is going to be powering the AI revolution the same way lithium, one in Li-ion batteries, has been crucial to creating minute batteries used in smartphones and tablets. Current materials are insufficient for powering the general AI, so keep an eye out for the discovery of one such mineral that will help us achieve massive computing speeds needed to make it a reality. If huge deposits of it happen to be found on the territory of one of these blocs, that one might become the 21st century's superpower; if that happens to be underdeveloped and unexplored Africa, that continent might just become the proving ground for every economic bloc to invade and fight over.

Chapter 8 – Seminal Inventions

We can take a look at seminal technological inventions to understand how they changed the way we do business and live our lives to extrapolate how AI will do the same. We can single out the internal combustion engine as the most significant invention that marked the twentieth century, driven by the use of fossil fuels. The internal combustion engine allowed us to travel faster for greater productivity and more leisure than ever before. Having a car soon became a status symbol and cities had to grow to accommodate them, paving over arable land and reserving plenty of usable space for parking to the point it is nearly impossible to do anything without a car.

The internal combustion engine also allowed us to have vans and trucks that haul cargo, providing us with unthinkable abundance, but also polluted our environment in a very palpable way; just take a look at any modern metropolis and the impenetrable veil of smog. Fossil fuels are an inconsequential pollution source, but it is when they became globally adopted, and everyone could afford a car, that they started seriously polluting. Ironically, they also made everyone richer, so there is no way to scale back and just "use less". Every bit of food we eat has to come through some form of transport that uses an internal combustion engine, meaning fossil fuels and pollution, and since the hunter-gatherer lifestyle is impossible in the city, we have to eat whatever is available, leading to all sorts of health problems in the long run.

Saudi Arabia, rich in fossil fuels, became a center of global power and grew from a tent city of camel herders to a glistening metropolis that can afford to build artificial archipelagos visible from space. The United States introduced the idea of the petrodollar and strongly suggested to every country to use US dollars exclusively to buy oil on the market. This created a high demand for US dollars, which could be printed to generate much more wealth than the US market could sustain on its own. Meanwhile, attempts to create an alternative to fossil fuels have failed, and it is only wishful thinking that makes countries install renewable energy sources, like wind turbines; in most cases, they are operating at a loss and have to be financed by the taxpayer.

Some random country might happen to have just the right ingredients to physically anchor AI in our world, suddenly making it an El Dorado. A shift in global power will be near instantaneous, tectonic and, due to the presence of nuclear weapons, surprisingly peaceful. It is likely that AI, once it reaches a sufficient level of penetration in our global digital society, will have the same impact the internal combustion engine had: more power, more productivity, more status, and more leisure. We did leave dedicated lanes for pedestrians (sidewalks) and forbade cars from driving on them; we also created dedicated lanes for cars (highways) and forbade pedestrians from walking on them. In computer terms, human legs are legacy hardware that is still supported in city infrastructure, so we will likely have to create an entirely new layer of infrastructure just to accommodate AI and leave the ordinary internet and landlines to humans.

It is not even a matter of willpower or societal organization; just compare the outputs of a tractor and a third-world village with hoes and shovels. A single machine driven by a human can do the work of

45

300 men, women, and children with ease while creating a tiny bit of pollution. Not just that, but the tractor driver is in a comfortable seat, with the cabin protecting him or her from the sun, so plowing is pleasant.

How likely is it that AI will leave people jobless? The same way we don't hear anyone complaining about tractors getting all the juicy plowing and hoeing jobs of villagers, AI will most certainly not remove jobs as they are but will automate and expedite certain simple, repeatable chores we had to do manually with great expense in time and energy. AI will make those chores more pleasant, and we'll be glad to have it finally, but there is also the problem of becoming too reliant on machines to the point we forget to use our brains.

Note how in the tractor analogy, it still mentioned "machine driven by a human". That wasn't just a figure of speech or a contrived circumstance—legally, all roadworthy vehicles have to be operated by a human, even in cases of horse carriages where an animal has a choice of speed and direction. Vehicles using an engine with internal combustion simply have to have someone accountable in case something goes wrong, meaning they have to be registered, serviced, and operators have to have a certain license, etc. If we compare a horse carriage driver to a car driver, we can clearly see that the increase in horsepower leads to a stricter licensing mandate. If AI ever becomes a household item, something each person will own just like we own smartphones, it is likely they will have to be licensed the same way some US states register guns in case something goes wrong.

Chapter 9 – Fear-based Consumerism

Humans are known to use performance boosters, nerve stimulants—such as coffee—that power the global economy. What is the equivalent to that when it comes to machines or AI? As far as we know, there is no such thing—meaning that machines may outperform humans but will have linear productivity at best and won't be able to keep up with humans that can constantly improve their performance, albeit temporarily. However, using performance boosters does have a drawback.

The alcohol crisis is skyrocketing in the US, especially with women. Responsible for the deaths of about three million people a year worldwide, alcohol is a brain stimulant that lowers inhibition and warps the sense of reality. Simply put, alcohol lets the user unwind and live in a slightly better world, even if excess use does cause a hangover the day after. The ultimate reason for wanting alcohol in the first place is stress—usually due to pushing the body to its utmost limits to keep going in the workplace. Entrepreneurs are particularly prone to pushing themselves and everyone around them through discomfort, lack of sleep, and pain, and we actually lionize them for it.

Being a well-rested entrepreneur is heresy even though sleep deprivation is a legitimate torture method that induces psychosis, a detachment from reality that fractures the mind. Presidents and leaders pride themselves in their autobiographies on making decisions without sleeping at all, even though they command armies and nuclear arsenals. How can we entrust the future of anything to a sleepless, crazed person who has barely had a good night's sleep in years? Yet, we have to have all these people, from common janitors to presidents, working themselves into an early grave or there is no chance to stay competitive in the global market. So, excessive demands and lack of sleep cause a tremendous deal of stress, the long-term breakdown of the body and psyche.

Caffeine abuse is another big problem when it comes to attempts to increase productivity without innovating or dealing with stress. We don't see coffee consumption as a problem—since it gives us that kick in the morning—but caffeine is a stimulant that hurts the body in the long run, particularly by disrupting sleep patterns, again compounding the problem of induced psychosis. Caffeine is not banned like heroin or cocaine only because it stimulates the economy. See the common theme? Whatever increases economic output is allowed.

All the executives working in tech giants are likely in such a psychosis induced by sleep deprivation and stimulant consumption that they have lost touch with reality and don't even know what they are doing, relying on the hierarchy of competent people below them to do their magic. In all likelihood, the fact tech giants' CEOs crave AI to take over is simply so—they can finally get a good night's rest. They are stressed out of their minds, but since all their projects are proprietary, nobody can tell if there is any truth to what they're saying regarding AI.

So, what is the real cause of stress? In engineering terms, stress is when a structure or an element in it is exposed to a certain amount of load; every beam, brick, and pillar have a certain range of load they can bear before breaking down. When it comes to humans, stress is a cognitive load caused when we perceive the world around us as dangerous and have to deal with the cause/s. Successfully doing so releases a small amount of feel-good chemicals in the brain that helps us unwind, making us feel accomplishment and satisfaction. If we can't deal with causes of stress, we develop coping mechanisms, such as finding comfort foods, highly caloric foods that typically have little nutrition but taste just right to trigger the release of same feel-good chemicals in the brain.

In a 2007 study titled "Stress, eating and the reward system"[22], a pair of University of California scientists researched the link between stress and indulging in comfort foods. In essence, stress is an evolved response to danger that triggers a short-lived "fight or flight" reflex, releasing adrenaline and cortisol that exhaust the body and shorten the lifespan. Stress is meant to give us superhuman strength so we can either fight back or escape danger, but the same stress response can trigger for no benefit during the course of an ordinary life, especially when you are involved in a dynamic work environment. So, if you're working in retail and a customer starts yelling at you, that causes your limbic system to think it is being attacked and triggers stress, causing you to either yell back (fight) or cower (flight).

The solution to stress is always to consider all situations as challenges rather than sources of danger. This simple change in perspective makes us use our neocortex rather than the limbic system, developing higher brain functions rather than triggering the most basic survival instincts. In essence, seeing a yelling customer as a challenge rather than a threat may let you reply with a witty remark that interrupts his or her angry rant and perhaps even makes them burst out laughing, turning a stressful situation into a relaxed and fun

---

22
    https://www.medicinasistemica.it/doc/biblioteca/Stress,%20eating%20and %20the%20reward%20system.pdf

one, where you can both work together to fix whatever problem there was without any stress.

The study examined how people who don't know about stress deal with it by eating caloric foods, such as cookies, that trigger a feel-good brain response just like a drug would; addiction to cookies can be purged from the brain using Naloxone, a medication that helps drug addicts kick their habit. It is not just that humans relieve stress this way because even rats exposed to extreme danger were eventually hooked on cookies or sugary water, which is the equivalent of soda or fruit juice. Who ultimately benefits from the general public being constantly stressed out? Companies that produce and market these stress-coping mechanisms, whether it is food, alcohol, medication, or some other vice that slowly ruins the body.

In essence, our very existence involves small amounts of stress from time to time but being included in a thriving financial market mandates that we are constantly stressed out, or we won't be giving our best to make and spend as much money. Big companies from media to food and entertainment have to whip us into a stress-fueled frenzy constantly, or we will just be happy with what little we have on our own and lead a peaceful life. Therefore, if tech giants decided they need the ultimate economic booster, they might announce a threat to end all threats—AI, a mystical and intangible perfect worker, advisor, lover, and warrior.

We don't have to take any heed of tech giants' AI doom and gloom announcements—since now we have an alternative explanation as to why they would be pushing it so intensely. Humans have always adapted to life and will continue to do so, except now you know that it is all just a challenge that can be solved using higher functions that lie dormant in the brain, being constantly overridden by the limbic system when we are stressed out fearing for our lives, which makes us utterly predictable and ultimately complacent. There is no external factor that can mold our behavior against our free will, as long as we are aware of the possibilities and consciously build our own path in life.

Looking at AI from a stress-free perspective of a human that doesn't feel fear, anxiety, anger, or hunger, what is the chance it will replace said human? No chance at all. Humans can exchange information and learn at a much faster rate than any machine as long as they are not using that pesky primal part of the brain, the limbic system, that always simplifies things.

Chapter 10 – AI and Growth Hacking

To use AI, you should first clearly define the goal and how it is going to be achieved using machine learning. You will be using what is known as "growth hacking", an entrepreneurial paradigm that relies on building a sturdy framework with repeatable steps you can always go back to if you get stuck. Just like a vine finds the nearest point to latch onto but always keeps climbing up to reach more sunlight, you too should improvise daily implementing AI while staying true to your ultimate goal.

Growth hacking relies on having steady sources of data and reliable ways of analyzing it. More than anything else, growth hacking means you will be having a scientific approach to whatever your project entails, without any kind of prejudice as to what the customers want or what the final product should look like. It is only after the data has been gathered and dissected to reach an actionable solution that you'll be using a tiny spark of creativity to find a new vantage point and climb up higher, just like the vine, to repeat the process all over again. Only after you have managed to do this kind of growth hacking independently of any AI is when you can actually afford to employ it. AI should always be used *to automate existing processes* that we know can produce working results but lack time or the workforce to iterate them enough times.

AI works in mysterious ways and might be offering solutions that fall within the bounds of statistical error. Therefore, be prepared to tweak your use cases and experiment with them until you have been fully satisfied with the answer. At first, try to simplify your questions so they can be answered with "yes" or "no" and have as many people participate in answering each question. Don't rush anything and just establish a sturdy foundation. The growth you experience shouldn't be sudden or explosive but controlled and manageable, or the unexpected success will overwhelm you.

Chapter 11 – AI and Correcting Fake News

Making news is an ordeal, which is why so many websites use clickbait, but at least they are not outright lying with the intent to influence elections. On the other hand, making fake news is fairly easy, and, with the help of gullible users on social media, spreads like wildfire to influence countries in the long run. China already has a solution—fact-checking bot Meiyu[23] that idles with users on social media and automatically corrects whatever they are saying in chats.

Described as being "Taiwanese" rather than Chinese, the bot is free—it is supposedly there to cite an open source database when a dubious article is mentioned and is not designed to collect personal data on users. However, it has to sift through user messages, getting access to all the data they mentioned in order to understand the conversation. All it has to do is create a report on who is the one spreading fake news for a friendly visit from the police.

If the bot is free, what is the motivation for the owner to even create it in the first place? The most likely answer is that the Chinese

---

23   https://outline.com/KD9TM6

government funded Meiyu; in particular, counter-intelligence services under the guise of venture investment, which is something that already happens in the US. The second most likely answer is that it hoovers up private data to create psychological profiles and sells them to advertising companies. Finally, it might also genuinely be made by a small-fry developer who has the best intentions, in which case actors from the previous two cases can still swoop in and buy the app, getting the entire user base and all the gathered data, even if it is only error reports.

Users didn't like Meiyu, especially when elders were in the chat— since disagreeing with an elder is considered in bad taste. Meiyu ultimately seemed more like a contrarian bot than a fact-checking one, simply barging into the conversation random assertions regardless of whether there was any truth to the material. For example, Meiyu disagreed that flu symptoms can be lessened by drinking more water, stating, "The internet has a lot of information on drinking water. Doctors say not all of it is credible."

Chapter 12 – AI and Big Data

When humans interact with a digital device, they leave behind a trace of information that is like a blip on a radar; with enough blips, a human can be reliably tracked down to the tiniest detail, and all it takes is a single fact-checking app. At the app developer's headquarters, an array of machines quietly vacuums in all possible data from users who have the app installed, including their text messages, phone numbers, Wi-Fi network names to triangulate location, and so on. Without even realizing it, users' smartphones become spying devices, and that is when the developer doesn't want to collect data. If a tech company wants to collect data, it can create special systems that are designed to label and sort data in a way that shields the company owner from liability but still allows full-blown surveillance.

Like tiny grains of sand on their own are imperceptible but piled up create a sand dune that can no longer be swept under the rug, bits of data can be piled up to create a monumental collection of user details and habits that reveal their most private thoughts and secrets. In essence, this is Big Data, an array of user data that is so big and keeps growing so fast that no human can keep it in check. Big Data is used to feed and perfect machine learning, which then helps build up Big Data even more. What can humans do against Big Data? Quite a bit, actually.

If you own a company that might collect user data, be advised that Big Data makes a juicy target for hackers, who can always find cheap, easy, and low-tech ways to breach security. The best defense against hackers is to: a) gather only minimum user data, b) delete all user data as soon as it is no longer needed and c) compartmentalize all data so a hacker can't get it all at once. This approach is called security by design and involves creating the simplest possible services and products with the fewest number of moving parts. Couple this with defense in depth, where physical access control is buttressed with software protections, meaning you keep data encrypted and locked in a secure room where only trusted people get the key. Make regular backups on dedicated hard drives and keep them disconnected from the internet.

If you are a programmer working for a company gathering Big Data, keep in mind that in the vast majority of cases, users of any service or product go with default settings. Whatever you set as the default is what your users will use without checking or even knowing how to change settings. Also, beware of "feature creep", where products get pivoted to take on more roles than they can realistically fulfill, making them vulnerable to hacking.

If you are a user who wants to keep their data out of Big Data, start lying. Whenever you're asked for personal information, such as name, e-mail, and date of birth, input fake responses—unless you're actually going to use those services—and delete old accounts that you are not using when they're being used to send you spam e-mails. Create burner e-mail accounts and choose long passwords for everything; password length is the best indicator of its strength, so don't bother with capital letters, numbers and special unless the product explicitly demands those. If you really need to use social media, use a separate device for each platform, and reset the devices to clear all personal data if you are going to give or sell them.

Chapter 13 – AI and Employment

In the current business environment in the US, IQ tests are forbidden as they lead to what is known as "disparate impact", which essentially means a business can get sued if it filters out incompetent people. Even when there is an actual need to have an employee with a set of skills, the employer can still get dragged through courts and thrown to the media court of opinion, so most of them just sigh and hire people who barely contribute to the business alongside actually productive employees. This practice of hiring token employees just to follow an idealistic notion of a perfect pie chart, where every racial and national identity gets a slice, is simply unsustainable and likely harmful, but employers do it anyway simply to avoid getting flak from the media.

In one such case that ended up in front of the Supreme Court, Ricci v DeStefano[24], a group of New Haven, Connecticut firefighters were jockeying for lieutenant and captain positions by passing a lengthy, costly exam. City authorities eventually threw out the results because not enough minority candidates passed the exam and the firefighters who should have gotten the promotion sued. The Supreme Court

---

24   https://www.supremecourt.gov/opinions/08pdf/07-1428.pdf

ruled that "race-based action like the City's in this case is impermissible under Title VII unless the employer can demonstrate a strong basis in evidence that, had it not taken the action, it would have been liable under the disparate-impact statute." In short, the exam was the best New Haven had, and that is what should have been used.

Imagine the state of affairs where firefighters respond to a call but have no clue how to proceed because they have all been hired based on their skin, eye or hair color rather than the actual ability to save lives and property. Rather than hiring the strongest, most athletic and resourceful people, firefighting becomes a process of quenching the fires of social discontent where politicians jostle for favorable media coverage by pandering to the most basic of tribal urges. Those who dare point out the problem get lambasted in the media, no matter how they framed it or how right they are. However, there is no negotiating with an open flame that is truly indiscriminate in whom it roasts.

Employers can't even refuse to hire or outright fire a pregnant woman, even if her job involves handling toxic materials that might affect the fetus. Some 75% of all women with employment in the US will become pregnant during their career, forcing the employer to: a) write off any costs on hiring and training the woman, b) pay for any costs incurred, as pregnancy is considered a chronic health problem and c) find a replacement for the pregnant woman at their own expense.

This stems from a Federal Pregnancy Discrimination Act of 1978[25], brought about by another Supreme Court case where a pregnant woman sued General Electric because its disability insurance program didn't cover pregnancy or childbirth. Courts all the way up to the Supreme Court affirmed that General Electric did no wrong because its disability program provided the same benefits to men and

---

25   https://legaldictionary.net/pregnancy-discrimination-act/

women, which is why Congress promptly adopted the Act to plug that neat loophole.

Compare this outcome to how Chinese businessmen would handle it—they would gladly send pregnant women through the grinder by the truckload if that meant a minimal increase in productivity of their factories, and the Chinese government would approve. Do you now see why so many companies moved their manufacturing to China? Thanks to minimal worker rights and maximum profit, China is the perfect place to experiment with any new kind of business product. If AI really is coming and is going to displace human workers, it would make sense to leave manufacturing capability in the first world rather than ship it out, but that is not what's happening.

Foxconn is one especially egregious example, owning a massive factory campus in China where workers have their daily quota set out for them by the most productive echelon of workers—do better than that, and everyone else has to speed up or get fired. Everything from seating positions to worker interactions is strictly controlled and optimized. Workers that decide they can't take it anymore usually end it all by jumping off the nearest campus building, which prompted Foxconn management to install safety nets that will make unhappy workers rethink their choices and deal with the shame of being fired. Foxconn produces some 40% of all consumer electronics used globally, such as Playstations, iPhones, Nintendo 3DS, and Xbox.

The Western idea of workplace equality, where pregnant women and minorities get a cushy job position just because of anti-discrimination laws, seems idealistic and quaint in a way that a philosopher, who has never run a successful business, would imagine it being run; China is more efficient in every given aspect, though it produces immense suffering. Businesses can't stay competitive if they have to deal with a constant barrage of complaints, lawsuits, and negative media headlines, which is why they generally create Human Resource (HR) departments to handle employee matters internally.

HR deals with hiring and firing, acting like a thought-police that micromanages employees' behavior to minimize legal liability for the employer. After the #MeToo scare, during which various women made claims of being sexually harassed by powerful men, Netflix's HR department introduced a rule that a male and female worker can't hold eye contact for more than five seconds at a time[26]—since that is what "invokes powerful sexual desire". Can HR do that? HR can do as it wills.

HR handles job interviews with its own byzantine schemes, which are specifically designed so the potential employee can't file a discrimination lawsuit. If you ever had the displeasure of suffering through six increasingly complex job interviews by the same company only to get rejected without a reason, now you know why—you were never considered for the job position in the first place, but the company had to put up a dog and pony show to minimize the chance of negative media coverage. The same thing goes with resumes, which are simply sent to the recycle bin save a select few—again chosen through "unknown divination rites".

However, what if an AI could do the hiring instead of HR? Incapable of discrimination or racial bias, which is what supposedly makes businesspeople avoid hiring minorities, an AI would be perfectly objective and always find the perfect employee without any need for an HR department. AI could also sift through Facebook and LinkedIn profiles to find upcoming talent and hire it before anyone else, snapping up all the hottest employees for peanuts before they know their worth. An AI could be able to find a suitable job for everyone, ensuring nobody goes hungry or destitute, which would boost the economy, eliminate unemployment, and solve the problem of prison recidivism. Sound like a great future?

26

http://exclaim.ca/film/article/netflix_allegedly_told_staff_not_to_make_eye _contact_for_more_than_5_seconds

Amazon actually tried making the perfect AI recruiter, but the results scared the engineering team working on it, and the project was quickly shut down—their digital brain consistently favored men over women, and there was apparently no way to tweak it without ruining it completely. Amazon's emphasis was on automation, with the idea that an executive could feed the neural network 100 or more resumes to get the five most qualified people for the position[27]. This kind of tool is a Holy Grail for all tech giants, as it would eliminate plenty of overhead related to hiring, but this project shows just how much progress we would have to undo. Right now, we all have to rely on a friend or relative to skip over the HR department anti-lawsuit moat, but the tool promised a bright future where nobody has to write or read a single resume.

By using a training dataset that consisted of ten years' worth of resumes, mostly those of men, Amazon's job candidate finder neural network picked up on some 50,000 keywords related to productivity. The tool learned that any resume with the word "women" or "women's" negatively affected that person's productivity. In addition, job candidates from all-women's colleges were extra penalized. Even after engineers made the tweak so that women were equal to men, the neural network was able to bypass the restriction and find another way of detecting if the resume belonged to a woman, penalizing it regardless. So, how did the tool evaluate resumes? Skills that were common among resumes were given low importance, such as the ability to write computer code. Aggressive, manly terms, such as "executed" and "captured", were given higher importance as they showed ambition and remorselessness.

What is interesting is that Amazon's tool recommended that unqualified candidates be given all sorts of job positions, which made engineers think it was just glitching and giving random results. However, the hiring process companies use right now relies on

27   https://www.theguardian.com/technology/2018/oct/10/amazon-hiring-ai-gender-bias-recruiting-engine

positive bias, meaning we expect better results from people who have provided similar results in the past, which makes sense but doesn't give a chance to people who have talent but haven't had the chance to get their foot in the door by going to a fancy university. The tool had no positive bias and recommended that Amazon introduces fresh blood at all levels because people without any experience have limitless potential. People who already have a filled-out resume have, in a sense, defined themselves, but naive schoolboys and girls could become anything and provide a novel perspective to any company's inner working.

It was a stroke of genius, one that can only be achieved by trawling through countless resumes and crunching trends to their constituent words and numbers to analyze them without the limbic system barging in. As companies grow, they mature from the startup phase, where they had to take a risk, to the corporate phase, where they wish to eliminate the risk that drove them in the first place. This makes established companies complacent, inert, and populated by all the same crusty executives that keep doing what their experience has taught them—except that is no longer enough in an eternally changing market. Of course, Amazon ignored this idea completely as an error and quietly shelved the entire project, but commented that it is committed to workplace diversity and equality because that is what the media want to hear.

Other companies are trying different approaches, mainly by analyzing facial expressions to see what the job candidate thinks of themselves. HireVue is a startup that assesses video interviews instead of resumes to reveal flashes of insight from unconscious facial expressions made by tiny muscles around the eyes and mouth. As you have probably figured out by now, this kind of analysis is probabilistic and works most of the time in some cases; we have no way of knowing if the candidate has had, for example, a root canal that would cause a painful grimace on the day of the video interview. It is an intriguing idea but still doesn't make the interviewing process fully automated.

LinkedIn would be the vanguard in AI hiring, so what does LinkedIn think of it? John Jersin, VP of the LinkedIn hiring department says, "I certainly would not trust any AI system today to make a hiring decision on its own" and "technology is just not ready yet." Well, that settles it. Transparency in AI-managed hiring processes is another problem—since there is no way to double-check the process or enforce workplace equality. There is already a term for this kind of problem: "algorithmic fairness".

The AI won't hire you based off of some goofy keyword shenanigans, but at least it won't throw you in jail, right? As it turns out, neural networks are already being used to jail people, especially those with a record of delinquency and/or a prior arrest record.

Chapter 14 – AI and The Legal System

Across the United States, different counties are experimenting with neural network tools that give criminals risk scores, a probability on a 1-10 scale if they will offend again. One exhaustive ProPublica article[28] describes a few cases of how this kind of software works and brings inside data about a prison system running on algorithms.

When Brisha Borden, an eighteen-year-old black girl, stole a bike for a joy ride on her way to school, she was arrested and charged with petty theft and burglary. Computer algorithm analyzing her record (four juvenile misdemeanors) gave her an 8/10, meaning she was very likely to repeat the crime. Meanwhile, Vernon Prater, a 41-year-old white man with one attempted and two performed armed robberies, got arrested for shoplifting from Home Depot and got rated a 3/10 by the same system. Two years later, Vernon attempted grand theft, but Brisha didn't do anything else, meaning the algorithm got it wrong. How come?

---

28   https://www.propublica.org/article/machine-bias-risk-assessments-in-criminal-sentencing

---

The human mind doesn't correctly understand probability and causes itself much grief in trying to figure out chances. When technology is introduced to the mix, it becomes an additional source of confusion because technology is never perfect. Just like you will see in a later chapter with a soap dispenser, technology is meant to work reliably with a certain acceptable range of inputs, but fringe cases may lead to it randomly failing. Furthermore, probabilities compound, so if we use inaccurate technology to double-check our guesstimate, the prediction will be much more inaccurate than if we just guesstimated. It sounds strange, but the math checks out.

Imagine setting up a police checkpoint to catch drunk drivers. Drunk driving is a wicked crime—one that could be completely prevented by self-driving cars that would kill the driver if need be—that endangers lives for no good reason, so we have a noble goal and feel good about inconveniencing drivers. Also imagine a state-of-the-art breathalyzer that has 99% accuracy. Sounds perfect, doesn't it? However, also assume that only one in a thousand drivers drive around drunk. What are the chances of catching the guy? Think carefully about the answer.

If you stop and test 1,000 drivers, the breathalyzer, which errs in 1% of cases, will show ten of them as being drunk while only one is actually drunk. Therefore, the breathalyzer has a 90% false-positive rate, and just falsely accused nine people of drunk driving. The worst part is that drivers will typically be so overwhelmed with guilt that they won't dare challenge the breathalyzer. It is state-of-the-art after all, so how could it possibly be making any mistakes, let alone so many? When coupled with something like SCS, a false drunk driving accusation can lead to a cascade of mishaps that completely ruins someone's life, and that is using a breathalyzer that's 99% accurate!

It turns out that, if an event isn't all that common, the technology used to detect it has to have a margin of error lower than the chance of incidence or there is no advantage to using the technology in the first place. In fact, the less common an event, the more wildly inaccurate the results of detection and prediction. You can play around with the incidence of drunk driving in this thought experiment, and you will see it is only when 90% of drivers drive drunk that the breathalyzer's margin of error equals the wrongful detection rate.

It turns out that humans are much more precise than technology; just imagine a breathalyzer that has 50% or less accuracy. The police and courts know how often false positives happen but press on regardless because the general public needs to see that something is being done about crime to appease their limbic systems, even though completely innocent people are being punished. This thought exercise also shows that all those mandatory drunk driving checkpoints are completely meaningless because we are inconveniencing 999 drivers to catch that one guy who is driving tipsy.

Therefore, this very simple thought experiment showed us that math is always the ultimate arbiter of efficiency that cuts through emotional nonsense and deprivation of human rights. You should always challenge the results of technology being used to prove something on the basis that: a) the operator wasn't skilled enough, b) technology can randomly fail and c) rare occurrences can't be reliably detected. Brisha's and Vernon's crime scores had nothing to do with the fact that she was a black girl and he was a white man, as the article subtly framed it, but most likely that petty theft happens much more often than armed robbery, which means the algorithm assigned it a much greater likelihood of happening again.

These algorithmic risk assessments are already used in courtrooms from Arizona to Wisconsin, with results given to judges during sentencing. The idea is to arrive at a number that shows how likely rehabilitation is going to work for any given defendant. In federal prisons, these kinds of assessments would become mandatory. As expected, political figures are latching on to "algorithmic unfairness" as an extension of systemic racism and bias, but it appears the explanation is much simpler than that—a tool used for risk assessment simply sucks.

Created by a for-profit company Northpointe, the crime prediction algorithm used to assess Brisha and Vernor was said to be proprietary and thus not available for examination. What we do know about it is that 137 questions were answered by either the defendant or pulled directly from their file, such as education level and current employment status. Created by a statistics professor, the company was later on sold for an undisclosed sum to another company. If this kind of tool becomes mandatory in courtrooms, someone will be making a ton of cash.

Previously, judges had plenty of leeway in how they wanted to treat the defendant, but political pressure to treat minorities better tied their hands—that is until they started using the risk assessment algorithms. Often attached as confidential documents during pre-sentencing to determine eligibility for probation, these scores were found to accurately predict recidivism about 61% of the time, with some variation depending on if the defendant was white or black. However, judges starting using them for sentencing, with some judgments even explicitly quoting the risk assessment score as the main reason for the harsh sentence. These have been challenged and successfully reduced. In Florida, Broward County uses the risk assessment score to determine if the defendant can be let out on bail, which the algorithm can also recommend to avoid jail overcrowding.

The risk assessment algorithm doesn't take into account that people can change for the better or that people have free will. It is actually quite easy to challenge the algorithm: if it's accurate, then free will doesn't exist, and the punishment makes no sense because the defendant's actions were predetermined; if it's not accurate, then it shouldn't be used at all—case dismissed, and the defendant is free to walk and might look into a career in law. The main way of fighting faulty technology is to challenge all conclusions drawn based on it, ask for insight into raw data based off of due process rights, and have a human expert or even the general public look into it.

Chapter 15 – AI and Self-driving Vehicles

A self-driving truck startup, Otto, sent one of its trucks on a 120-mile journey[29] to deliver 51,000 cans of Budweiser. Uber, which has already vowed to eliminate human drivers from its workforce, bought Otto and is now experimenting with self-driving vehicles as a part of a marketing tactic that is meant to impress investors. Pay attention to the details of the journey to see the flaws of self-driving vehicles.

With an empty driver's seat, the driverless truck was surrounded by four police vehicles and three Otto vehicles that were meant to intervene in case someone got thirsty, or the truck broke down; two tow trucks were plowing through traffic ahead to ensure nobody messed with the truck's trajectory. The driver lounged in the back but took control once the truck left the highway. Otto later confirmed that they did the same route before with a human driver at the wheel who never had to take control. Budweiser logistics manager explained that they eagerly want to see this kind of delivery method

---

29   https://money.cnn.com/2016/10/25/technology/otto-budweiser-self-driving-truck/index.html

scale. Shailen Bhatt, Colorado's Executive Director of the Department of Transportation, said that self-driving trucks are in a legal gray area, but the technology could at some point become as ubiquitous as automatic transmission. Neither Otto nor Budweiser manufacturer could elaborate on when they see self-driving trucks becoming a regular part of the traffic.

How many flaws did you spot? Driverless vehicles will need constant attention by humans, and in this case, a single car required attention from at least seven people (one driver per each vehicle surrounding it, not counting drivers in tow trucks) plus a driver in the back of the truck. So why is the driver there? Because the truck's sensors rely heavily on using immaculate highway traffic signs to navigate; once the truck is on dirt or gravel, the neural network driving it goes haywire.

Self-driving vehicles require an enormous infrastructure to work properly, and that is without humans interfering with it. It is quite likely human drivers encountering self-driving trucks would intentionally mess with it just for fun or to eke out a settlement, so there would again have to be a human driver in the cab just for optics. Companies that own and dispatch self-driving vehicles would then most likely push for human-free lanes, where neural networks have the right of way at all times and can form seamless convoys. How is that different from using a train to move cargo?

Further, self-driving vehicles are in a legally gray area, meaning they can't get insured or registered as regular vehicles can. It is unknown if self-driving trucks can scale, meaning we can sort of tell what happens if one self-driving truck is sent on a voyage but what happens if ten million are sent every which way at the same time? What kind of infrastructure would the logistics company need to build to manage that?

Plenty of things don't add up when it comes to self-driving trucks. Jumbo jets have had autopilot capability for some 40 years, but we still need a human pilot *and* a backup pilot, so self-driving trucks will by all accounts require more people to be hired. They obviously cost plenty of money and effort without an immediate return, so why are companies pushing for them? Without an apparent answer, the most likely reason is that there is a certain pride in being able to call one's own company fully automated.

Surveys done with potential self-driving car buyers showed that they overwhelmingly want a car that would destroy itself and its driver rather than kill the passers-by. The problem is, when they are asked if they would buy or drive that kind of car, they vehemently said, "No." The interests of tech giants to increase their reach and surveillance clash with societal norms, capabilities of neural networks, and even the human instinct for self-preservation stemming from the limbic system. Legal liability for this kind of thing would be enormous and no kind of suicide clauses in the purchase agreement would shield a tech giant from a flurry of lawsuits.

However, presenting the self-driving car as being operated by an AI that has been granted a status of deity could work as a legal loophole. There is already the precedent of "force majeure"[30] or higher force that allows companies to slip out of contracts, most notably in cases where numerous property insurance payouts would bankrupt the company. Force majeure is reserved for overwhelming events, such as riots and wars, but also includes elemental disasters, such as tornadoes and floods, that utterly destroy a certain area. Considered "an act of God", force majeure could be used after an AI has been presented as a deity, making it legally immune to lawsuits and contracts in cases of self-driving car pileups.

---

30   https://www.investopedia.com/terms/f/forcemajeure.asp

Chapter 16 – Tech Giants As Rulers of Society

Imagine an ancient tribe of natives living in the jungle that survive mainly on roots they dig out of the ground using their bare hands. Everyone spends most of the day digging for roots under the auspices of a wise tribe elder, the most experienced root finder who also enforces a **taboo**, an unspoken communal rule, passed from time immemorial, that says tribe members must not use any tools. When one young tribesman makes a simple shovel and shows how quick and easy it is to find roots, the elder is worried—this directly challenges his position of power, and the tribe is starting to wonder if perhaps the young upstart should lead the tribe.

So, the elder strikes a deal with the young tribesman: a special exception will be made in the taboo, allowing the use of a sacred tool in finding roots as long as the elder is the one wielding it; for the benefit of the tribe, of course. Further, the young tribesman will be given special honors for creating the shovel but must not challenge the taboo and must give a certain amount of roots he finds each day, so he doesn't start thinking of challenging the elder. Without having a better choice, the young tribesman agrees, secretly plotting for the day he will finally get to lead the tribe and set his own rules. The tribe doesn't care either way as long as the elder sanctions it and as long as they are kept fed and with enough time for leisure.

All of a sudden, the tribe's storeroom is bursting at the seams with roots. Everyone is given a task related to finding, processing, and storing roots, and they all get some root depending on the importance of their job and performance. Women have enough time to weave clothes from plants, and men get to make toys for children from rocks and musical instruments from wood. Life is good and easy. Naturally, the elder overseeing it all and handling the sacred shovel gets the best pick of roots. In a nutshell, this story explains how entrepreneurs challenge the established way of doing things but then get their work harnessed by politicians enacting laws and collecting taxes to power the economy and create prosperity for the entire tribe.

The same story plays out even today, except scaled up and with countless tribe members having a say in how things get done by voting. However, the fundamentals have remained the same— business success is offensive as it disturbs the established order of things and introduces *uncertainty* that upsets the tribe, which is why politicians haggle over the best way to control business success to get all the credit and make the tribe content.

It all comes down to getting votes, and all politicians ultimately vie for votes in the same way a tribe elder would—by celebrating the strength of the tribe, promising plenty of root hunting opportunities, having full storerooms of roots for everyone, and providing pretty clothes for women, fun musical instruments for men, and great toys for kids. Entrepreneurs aren't satisfied by these empty promises since their entire goal was fundamentally changing how the entire tribe leads its life; all they got were meaningless honors and tokens of appreciation. So, what do entrepreneurs want? A fundamental change for the better.

Successful people would give everything they have to help out the disadvantaged and never again have to deal with panhandlers begging for change. Why, aren't they the dreaded 1% who live in mansions and use secret Illuminati handshakes? Don't they gloat at the misery and degradation of the common man? Not at all. Successful people know the recipe to success and can repeatedly achieve it, but even if they gave away *everything*, they wouldn't be able to make an appreciable dent in overall poverty. Simply put, we have no idea how to fix things like generational poverty, where broken parents engender insecurity in their children through domestic abuse, making them drop out of school, develop anti-social behaviors, and become broken parents themselves.

All the best scientists put together can't figure out how to prevent the formation of psychopathic behavior, even if the warning signs are spotted in time. If little Johnny starts mutilating animals, there is a strong chance he will get into serious trouble as he enters his 20s, but no amount of intervention can halt or reverse this course of action. Attempts by sociologists to delay the formation of such a personality, for example, by putting Johnny in a pleasant environment with caring parents, have even been found to *aggravate* the problem. The best our society can come up with is to wait for Johnny to start making problems and then put him in jail, meaning closed quarters with all the other ruffians and psychopaths, giving them plenty of free time to learn advanced tricks of the trade from one another.

It appears personality is partly ingrained in the genetic code of each person and that the immediate sociological environment triggers the expression of an archetype, such as a warrior, poet or merchant, which is what Jung set forth as a fundamental psychological principle in his writings. We can't stop the expression of behaviors, but we can put them to good use through capitalism. With the example of little Johnny, getting him employed as a butcher all of a sudden productively harnesses his destructive urges, gives him respectable employment, and makes him a valued member of the community. Ultimately, entrepreneurs all want to shape society, so everyone has a worthwhile job, but see politicians as the main obstacle.

What if a certain group of entrepreneurs got together and started scheming how to displace politicians once and for all? By using technology, these upstarts would try to gather as much data on the behavior of the general public to understand how the mind works, why people vote the way they do, and so on. These tech giants would then try to create a digital nation populated by ethereal tribesmen, exact replicas of living people that would serve them without question, gloating at the imaginary clout they wield.

All the warnings about AI taking jobs and governments needing to introduce UBI aren't aimed at Joe Schmoe, truck driver, *but at politicians* who have no clue how technology works in order to make them yield to tech giants and acknowledge them as the ultimate tribe leaders. When a tech company announces their AI will take away jobs, they aren't giving out a kind-hearted warning but are actually threatening politicians: "Our technology will take away your ability to get votes by harnessing our effort." That is what it's all about, control of the society through uncertainty, not merely having a machine that can climb stairs, move boxes, flip burgers, or fold laundry on its own.

So far, AI has only proven itself useful in the narrowest sense of the word, such as when crunching data from resumes, making simple mechanical motions or comparing images, but hasn't come anywhere close to human intelligence. By the looks of it, AI won't be coming near human intelligence in the next 50 years—save for some revolutionary discovery that would make computers a million times faster than they already are. Right now, AI is like a shovel that tech giants say only they are allowed to build, inspect, and use, and according to their words, it is the best shovel anyone could ever dream of, so the tribe elder might as well scurry off into the jungle and let them lead the tribe. Why would they ever lie?

Chapter 17 – AI as One World Religion

When you have this kind of context, you can finally understand the political aspirations of tech giant CEOs, most notably Mark Zuckerberg, who all but admitted to running for president in the future 2020 US elections[31], his platform almost entirely focusing on UBI. In other words, free roots for everyone. So, how well would a country managed by Mark fare? Let's see how he is managing his own company for clues.

On March 13 2019, Facebook, Instagram, and WhatsApp had a massive worldwide outage[32]. Depending on users, some functions were available, but most others were down. Websites that use Facebook accounts for logins also had trouble with those functions. It took over a day before everything was in order, with the official explanation being "server configuration change," which doesn't exclude hackers since they too can change server configuration.

31   https://www.cnbc.com/2017/08/15/mark-zuckerberg-could-be-running-for-president-in-2020.html

32   https://www.theverge.com/2019/3/14/18265185/facebook-instagram-whatsapp-outage-2019-return-back

Now imagine Facebook's websites being the only ones existing on the internet, and you can see just how unfeasible that would be. One tech giant controlling much of the internet would make it extremely vulnerable to hacking attacks, but they will be pushing for the monoculture anyway because it is about political control, not increased productivity and user needs. This is quite like religious zealots talking about their religion as "the only right way". Technically a competitor to Google, Microsoft is adopting some of the same tactics and even some of the same software.

In 2018, Microsoft announced that its Edge browser was going to be powered by Google's Chromium engine, the same one used in Google Chrome. So users could pick between Edge or Chrome but would essentially get the same thing no matter what. Website creators would predictably take the easy way out and just optimize websites for Chromium, making other browsers less enjoyable to use and gradually nudging users into using Chrome.

The web-based Skype application recent update already made it work only in Edge and Chrome, proving that tech giants are more than willing to lock everyone else out of the fun. But hackers who tinkered with other browsers proved that the same update could be applied to other browsers if they falsely identify themselves as Edge or Chrome[33]. It is not that Microsoft can't make things work in Firefox or Safari; it's that it won't just to create a monopoly. That is particularly ironic since Skype is marketed as a way to bridge the gap across platforms and continents but actually funnels users into a monoculture world, where only those apps by the same company work seamlessly. This kind of behavior happened with Microsoft, and it will happen again, fueled by the executives' fear of losing market shares.

If AI is a deity, then who are the priests? Various scientists from all fields see themselves as the only ones worthy of interpreting the

---

33   https://arstechnica.com/gadgets/2019/03/microsofts-new-skype-for-web-client-an-early-taste-of-the-browser-monoculture/

ineffable will of the divine machine brain. In 2019, Stanford University unveiled a new institute dedicated to AI[34], but there was little mention of science and a whole lot of proselytizing. Rather than dividing humanity into nations that compete using AI, the institute presented the idea of a unified humanity. Led by Fei-Fei Li, Google's chief AI scientist at one moment, the Stanford Institute for Human-Centered Artificial Intelligence is slated to become the religion of the 21st century. So, a private organization run by a Google employee who just so happens to be Chinese.

Touting the coming of "Age of AI", promotional materials boast that AI will transform everything from law to medicine and literature. Of course, Stanford University will be the center of worldwide activity for lawmakers, politicians, and entrepreneurs, who will have to go there to ask for official approval before making any decision concerning humans. Comprised of staff broadly representing different nationalities and skin tones, the institute is meant to show humanity what it is like to cooperate on a global scale.

In theory, AI will know everything better than humans, but it is these scientists who will interpret its will, just like priests of pagan religions. AI will be described as being dangerous to the general public, which would necessitate its containment in the Stanford vaults, conveniently hiding all the raw data inputs and decision-making processes from being independently analyzed. Don't worry, people in power have never abused it, especially when they were as humble as these Stanford prodigies.

Tech giants were the ones behind this kind of AI-friendly movement, so it is no wonder they too want in on the action. In 2017, Google pivoted its marketing to be "AI first", rebranding the research department as "Google AI". There are dissenting voices, such as Steve Blank, a professor at Stanford, who said that people who develop new technology typically aren't held liable for its misuse

---

34   https://www.mercurynews.com/2019/03/15/stanford-unveils-new-ai-institute-built-to-create-a-better-future-for-all-humanity/amp

and mentioning that technology always has consequences beyond anything its creators imagine.

Chapter 18 – Dietary Advice by AI

Diet is going to be one of those areas where AI helps dish out useful information so each person can step up to the plate that fits him or her genetically. Imagine replacing white bread with a 40-60 corn and rye one that tastes weird but finally solves your bloating, acne, and rashes. For whatever reason, changing something in the diet helps tremendously with health problems, but we typically never consider the option consciously or know what to do about it. Plenty of foods we are eating have nothing to do with our needs but are rather a force of habit or a yearning for comfort food due to excess exposure to stress.

When it comes to food, current market conditions require uninformed customers with low impulse control to achieve financial growth—just look at how gluten turned out. Typically found in nature as a wheat protein that functions like glue to keep the seed in one piece, gluten was isolated and put into commercial use as a thickener sometime in the early twentieth century—used in ice creams to stop them from melting too quickly. Isolated gluten acts like a tiny bullet in the human digestive tract, poking holes which heal up quickly; overuse of gluten over *decades* leads to severe intestinal problems and autoimmune diseases in consumers.

Companies used gluten because it made foods chewy, replaced more expensive ingredients without the product falling apart, and increased shelf life. Food safety inspectors didn't find any problem with gluten because they were typically underfunded and overworked; without any evidence to the contrary, gluten was allowed on the market, which opened the floodgates to wanton experimentation with all sorts of substances. Meanwhile, a typical consumer sees a cheaper ice cream that melts slower, and tastes chewier than the competition because it has gluten; who cares if it's the real thing or it harms health? It was only about a century later that the ruse was discovered and everyone started freaking out when the limbic system kicked into high gear, but by that time, food companies had made a fortune *selling inferior products under the guise of quality*.

What is interesting about gluten is that it has a different impact on different individuals, with exposure in youth, apparently, activating certain genes that lead to health problems later in life. It is hard to speak in certainties when it comes to gluten because the human digestive tract is so complex that elucidating just one process in it deserves—and usually gets—a Nobel Prize. In the end, use of gluten in foods turned out to be an extensive experiment on the general public devised by food companies, sanctioned by the government, and funded by the oblivious consumer driven by the limbic system. Why? *Because it increased economic growth* through an increase in food sales and consumption.

There is no reason to believe the deployment of AI in any society will fare any better than the deployment of gluten. However, gluten could be blended seamlessly with other ingredients, but AI will stick out like a sore thumb, mandating that we willingly accept and adore it from the start. That is another explanation as to why so many influential people have started advocating for AI, despite it being well off in the future. Mass adoption of AI will require wholesale enlightenment, total turnover in how companies do their business *or both*; most likely neither will happen but let's examine the possibilities regardless.

According to a *New York Times* article[35], where the reporter, also a cardiologist, used an app to log everything he ate, and how much he slept and exercised over fourteen days, AI can make us seriously doubt what we have been eating all our lives. Alongside a sensor that tracked his blood sugar levels, the reporter also had his stool analyzed for gut bacteria to see what was inside his intestines; different people have different bacteria in their gut, with each strain liking different foods.

Most food studies are observational and voluntary, meaning they rely on participants to report what they have been eating over the years correctly. The best possible diet study results show correlation, but we have no idea about cause and effect, except when it comes to salt—excessive use over the years definitely increases blood pressure. Who funds the most dietary research? The same food industry that is interested in peddling as many cheap and stable replacements for genuine ingredients it can find. Is there an optimal diet for all people? We have no idea, which is why AI is meant to sift through all the data of people with a similar genetic profile, analyze how they fared on certain diets, and bring us probabilistic recommendations.

Everything from family history to toxins in the environment and gut bacteria plays a role in how the body processes foods. From time to time, there is a landmark study with promising results that tries to isolate that one key factor, but then it gets challenged, and conclusions are softened up. One such study was "Personalized Nutrition by Prediction of Glycemic Responses", which looked at how blood sugar levels of participants spiked in response to 52,000 of the most popular foods, including ice cream.

Posited to be a major predictor of diabetes, blood sugar level spikes ("glycemic responses" from the study title) mean the body has to strain to process the food it just ate. Apples and hazelnuts have a low

---

35   https://www.nytimes.com/2019/03/02/opinion/sunday/diet-artificial-intelligence-diabetes.html

glycemic index, but refined sugar and soda have a high one; in general, more refined foods act as more of a shock on the body. 800 people with diabetes had their glucose levels measured until the scientists got over 1.5 million measurements, after which it was time for AI to crunch it all without human bias. Gut bacteria were found to be the most significant factor in how individuals reacted to different foods. After that, the reporter got the chance to try out the system for himself—all recommendations by the AI were foods the reporter hated, and all foods to avoid were what he enjoyed the most.

Commercial versions of the same AI, though simplified, are meant to use pictures of a person's plate to identify foods and make recommendations to avoid laborious manual reporting of foods, but without measuring glucose levels, preferably through a medical wearable, it is all just slightly better than a random guess. In the reporter's case, he had kidney stones that were exacerbated by foods like strawberries, which the dietary AI coach recommended.

For now, we have universal diets like Paleo and Keto. The Paleo diet says that processed foods hold many nasty surprises, and each link in the processing chain can taint the food before it lands on our plate. So, the Paleo diet recommends eating "clean" foods, meaning those you know for certain how they were grown, stored, and processed. If possible, grow your own fruit, veggies, and poultry. The Keto diet aims to deal with blood glucose spikes by avoiding refined carbohydrates or just carbohydrates in general, meaning no bread, candy, sugar or soda and just a bit of fruit a day. The Keto diet has been found to stop epileptic attacks that no medication can subdue; science still has no idea why that happens.

Chapter 19 – AI and Loneliness

It seems that in the future loneliness will be the biggest problem as we interact with one another through screens rather than in person. The problem arises because our brain is primed for receiving subconscious cues from other people that make us more aware of our surroundings and our social context, bringing us in touch with reality; without those cues, this vast neural machinery starts shutting down. Despite there being a potential for positive and negative experiences out in the real world, at least they are real in the true sense of the word and elicit some kind of maturity, but the digital ocean of clickbait experiences online aims for the lowest common denominator in our personalities to trigger fear, anxiety, and panic to keep us online for as long as possible.

It has been known that isolation warps the mind, and extreme isolation can cause hallucinations and panic attacks, which is why solitary confinement is a real punishment for even the worst criminals. A series of experiments[36] with sensory deprivation done on Canadian students had them fitted with an elaborate array of

36   http://www.bbc.com/future/story/20140514-how-extreme-isolation-warps-minds

wearables designed to minimize brain stimulation: mufflers over the ears, blindfolds over the eyes, etc. After a few hours, students began showing restlessness, and past that, they started wildly hallucinating, seeing bizarre scenes that differed from one person to the next. Their mental performance degraded, and they couldn't shake off the feeling that they were in a weird dream, with the room and objects in it spinning or changing shape well after they regained stimulation. None of them managed past the two-day mark.

The reason for this is that the human brain is designed to absorb and process a massive volume of data, with any dearth in volume impacting it negatively; it is like a car that breaks down if it slows down, but the parts retain the inertia for a bit and spread out even when the car is no longer moving. Prolonged isolation makes for a tragic life, one where the brain gradually starts adapting to the solitude by making up elaborate fantasies and detailed worlds, often peppering them with imaginary visual experiences. When baby monkeys are isolated from the group, after 30 days they become completely unable to function with their brethren, their brains having been deprived of stimulation at their most vulnerable; children who go through the same become socially stunted to the extreme.

Entrepreneurs also experience isolation as they abandon their social circle and family to chase business success. It is a willing sacrifice, one that numbs the mind and makes the entrepreneur unfeeling and uncaring, with a laser focus on the goal that ignores everything else. Later on, entrepreneurs overcompensate by indulging in lavish physical pleasures, but the simplest of human interactions simply aren't there daily to keep their social circuitry running.

Prisoners experience the worst kind of isolation, as their only human contact is with other prisoners and guards, both of which generally give them a hard time. In some cases, prisoners forgo any manners and adopt total aggression because they have lost that nuanced social calibration that comes through constant social contact. What do we do with these people? Do we just let risk assessment neural networks decide their fate, even if they recommend keeping them locked up in isolation, or do we keep trying to find a solution that will ultimately rehabilitate them, as bizarre as that might be?

A common coping mechanism for persons in isolation is to find a higher, more abstract meaning to life. Rather than focusing on worldly pleasures, they can start to take joy in creating art, reading, or solving math equations. Religion helps as well, which is why monks retreat to the mountains for decades with scarce human contact as that lets them hear the word of God. All starting to make sense now? It is likely that entrepreneurs experiencing the same lack of human contact also start developing the same psychoses, making them think AI is coming.

What makes isolation all the more tragic is that so many people sentence themselves to voluntary solitary confinement, opting for the pristine digital world instead of the messy physical one without having any entrepreneurial leanings to at least get a source of income up and running. Without human contact and a source of income, social skills wane, and the person becomes unable to keep eye contact or have a meaningful conversation without self-doubt. If there is a physical problem as well, in particular, one that impacts mobility, the person has no money to fix it and loses the social circle for good. It is a self-compounding problem that requires extensive rehabilitation, which might as well be done by AI. In theory, if a general AI was made and available to the general public right now, what would be an easy and scalable solution to both personality problems and consequences of isolation?

An AI could assess psychological risks in each individual and devise a personalized approach that would lead to behavioral improvements. One such AI could also present itself as the word of God to those eager to hear it and have its messages delivered through an IoT ecosystem that made them pervasive and inescapable. By giving small challenges to the person, the AI would slowly shift their brain into a higher gear and make them a functional part of society, also teaching them a thing or two about social calibration. Aggression wouldn't scare the AI, who wouldn't have the limbic system that panics in order to survive. With limitless patience and infinite wisdom, this word of God could slowly reprogram the person to become happy and more productive. Sounds too scary? Frankly, we have no other solution for anti-social personalities that have been thoroughly destroyed by lack of care and emotional connection.

Knowing a person's past and having access to digital records, the AI could take on the voice of an authority or just a relative the person will yield to. Failing that, the voice can simply be made to be as soothing as possible, lulling the limbic system into complacency. If that kind of system is added to the existing healthcare infrastructure, nurses and doctors get more time to deal with waves of paperwork and layers of administration. Coupled with the fact that chronic health problems require an entire network of carers to handle just one patient, we will most likely be needing AI—stat.

An AI could be chatting with patients to keep them occupied while assessing their vocabulary, mental illnesses, or just general mood, producing a handy report for the doctor who can get the whole picture without wasting any time. The AI could automatically feed anonymized data to a database that would update it in real time, showing incidence in different kinds of strokes, injuries, cancers, and so on, which could help politicians develop health strategies as problems occur rather than twenty years after.

Chapter 20 – AI and Ethics

Images and X-rays could be analyzed by this medical AI, which could peer into the image down to the very last pixel to see the earliest signs and the possible spread of disease. For those with phobias and anxiety, virtual reality goggles could be supplied where an AI would walk them through the trauma and give them the right instructions on how to handle the situation down to the tiniest detail. When used with video call software, such as Skype, AI could analyze bedridden patients' faces to read into their inner world better than any human could. There should be informed consent by patients, who should at all times be aware that they are speaking with a machine rather than a human, but seeing how major social networks have been confessing they literally spy on users, and nobody batted an eye, it is likely patients would go with the program.

Doctors have much leeway in how they handle patients and might have to resort to extreme measures to handle extreme cases. It is not malice or arrogance but the need to be efficient and avoid emotional attachment to the patient, both of which are accomplished by going with the quickest solution, usually some form of prescription medication. However, doctors also have a code of ethics that can best be summed up as "first, do no harm". What if an AI was required to do some sort of an extreme measure to save a patient's life? Would AI then need the same code of ethics doctors have to stop it from going mad scientist on hapless patients?

According to Stuart Russell[37], author of a book on AI, we are facing a future where smart machines absolutely have to be given a mandatory code of ethics as they can produce fake news to change our voting and spending behavior. They can already trawl social media to pick up on keywords to determine personality traits and then perform automated chatting, espionage, and blackmail. Stuart also created "Slaughterbots"[38], a dramatized video on how tiny drones could be used for assassination in preparation for his petition to ban autonomous weapons in front of the United Nations. Capable of avoiding lazy swats, the drone can literally dive-bomb a target, delivering three grams of explosives right at the center of the forehead for instant death.

While dramatic, the Slaughterbots video doesn't explain how it is fighting off autonomous drones any worse than, say, fighting off swooping magpies that aggressively defend their nests during nesting season in Australia[39]. Humans have been dealing with murderous animals, including deadly insects and rampaging predators, for millennia, but drones would also presumably be extremely vulnerable to something like a nerf gun or a super soaker. It is easy to imagine humans making a sport out of hunting down these assassin drones while using special goggles to see them and wearing headcams to stream this first-class entertainment. Well, that is what humans do.

---

37   https://www.wbur.org/onpoint/2018/01/09/does-artificial-intelligence-need-a-code-of-ethics

38   https://www.youtube.com/watch?v=9CO6M2HsoIA

39   https://www.youtube.com/watch?v=YGGTcYfrEZU

So, drones could have ethical behavior baked into their programming, and the government could oversee ethical standards just like it does electrical and engineering ones. Isaac Asimov already thought of the idea of robots having ethical rules, namely with his three laws of robotics that can be summed up as: 1) don't hurt human, 2) obey human, and 3) preserve yourself. The problem arises when we think of traditional programming that ignores context and how AI could interpret any such ethical restrictions. If a human is taking a walk, should a smart machine forbid it because sunlight causes skin cancer? How about if a human wants to drive in a car or go skydiving?

The question of ethical limitation can be posited as: how much power do we want machines to have over us? Too much and we are serfs in a prison of our own construction, so it appears that the answer is giving the machines enough consciousness to recognize when we are making bad choices but not enough power so they can stop us from making them. We want smart machines to be our advisors that will gather raw data, present it transparently, and crunch the numbers to a simple conclusion with such clarity that it stands up to every possible challenge but ultimately leave the choice to us. Even when they hurt, wrong choices typically lead to valuable lessons that last for a lifetime.

Chapter 21 – AI and Social Credit

While the US might be leading in AI research, it is China that does most of the implementation on a large scale. China can leverage its massive population to both produce a large volume of engineers and train any sort of neural network as a diverse set of challenges. Just like we can see with the simplest products, the Chinese have no shame when it comes to copying what smarter people have already done and just toying with it using their extremely cheap workforce to make a working prototype and turn it into profit. In fact, big US companies might want to tap into the Chinese market just to sip from that fount of data and leverage the workforce to iterate on a product that would then be offered to the US market, under the auspices of the Chinese government of course.

Google already made inroads into China as a search engine of choice from 2006-2010 but gave up because of extreme censorship demands, hacking attacks, employee interrogations, and theft of intellectual property[40]. In 2018, Google decided to give it another try, which startled analysts who stated that, if anything, the Chinese government made the online environment much more hostile so

---

40   https://www.wired.com/2010/01/google-censorship-china/

there must be some really pressing concern that made Google so eager to enter China.

According to Dr. Kai-Fu Lee, the former president of Google China, we are entering the age of AI where "data is the new oil, and China is going to be the new Saudi Arabia" and workers won't simply be displaced by machines in a 1:1 ratio—entire industries will be automated and people depending on them disenfranchised. He calls for some form of income redistribution since companies employing AI will easily earn billions of dollars, so charging them extra tax seems like the most natural solution but argues against UBI as presented in the media.

Dr. Lee says that governments around the world will have to provide citizens with "meaning to life" more than just the means to live and mentions that jobs where the outcome has more to do with human satisfaction rather than 0s and 1s, such as nannies and teachers, are still safe from automation. Creative creators, for example, writers and painters, also have nothing to fear for quite a long time. For many people, says Dr. Lee, work is the meaning of life, and they expect to have the same old routine for 60 years of their existence just like their forefathers, so having that snatched away from them won't put them in a good mood.

The thing is, we are already treating our workers as robots: sit still, fill out these spreadsheets, and send them out in an e-mail for eight hours a day, so automating their jobs will actually be doing them a favor. How about giving them a smart tool that fills out the spreadsheets, and they just double-check the results? That would absolve the company of any legal liability as there would still be a human, but the work output could increase tremendously, though with some reduction in overall quality. It is telling that two countries with the feeblest consumer protection laws, the United States and China, are the ones pushing for AI as their captive customers have very little say in what they get.

This common ground could be used to let Chinese-style censorship enter the US through tech giants, such as Facebook and Google, which have already expanded to the point they resemble nation states, except they can't be defeated in a war. China's social credit system (SCS) is like a huge video game, save that the consequences of being low on the scoreboard mean being shut off from government essentials, such as education and public transport. What causes loss of social score? Traffic accidents, murders, embezzlement, and being related to someone who did any of those.

In one instance in 2015, a young Chinese student, Zhong Pei, couldn't buy a train ticket or enroll at a university because her dad had killed two people and himself in a car accident[41]. The official label entered in the system was that Pei was "dishonest", but she was able to clear her name after four months. Already built and trialed by Tencent and Alibaba, the Chinese equivalents of Apple and Amazon, SCS will become China-wide in 2020, where everything a citizen does will go into figuring out their score. Drinking, playing video games too much, or simply hanging out with the wrong people? SCS will consider whether hobbies, purchases, and health habits deviate from what the Party has set out for a model citizen to dole out the punishment: social and economic isolation. The only problem is, as we saw with the Canadian isolation experiments, those measures radicalize people and warp their sense of reality.

The idea behind SCS is that the Chinese government can't possibly handle over a billion people who might own powerful technology, so untrustworthy ones most likely to cause trouble should be identified and gradually squeezed out of the big cities, including those who could help them claw their way back in. According to that logic, SCS will reward those who act responsibly while acting as a pre-punishment to those who endanger themselves and others. Other punishments include the cutting off internet access, no access to

---

41   https://katusaresearch.com/chinas-social-credit-system-coming-to-united-states/

housing loans or job opportunities, and a revoked passport. What will those people do to survive in a world with increasingly hostile technology?

Chapter 22 – Hacking AI

The idea of hacking refers to having a cheap, scalable, and reliable way of introducing uncertainty into any computer system to produce an unexpected result. Because of how they are programmed, computer systems typically fail catastrophically when faced with unacceptable inputs. One example of this would be buffer overflow, which is when something like a text box on a website allows any visitor to input any number as age; a hacker can tinker with inputs until he or she finds such a strange number that it crashes the website or gives them total access to the backend.

Usually being rushed to production, websites and software don't check for all possible inputs or even restrict them because just getting things to run at all takes so much time and effort. At least after a hacking attack, the owner of the software or website will plug the hole, right? In computer systems that are large enough, the owner might not even have the resources or willpower to keep fixing these code loopholes, leaving the customers to fend for themselves. In cases where the system has been silently infiltrated in a way that doesn't cause the customer to notice, the owner might even willingly ignore it and focus on those problems that might lead to a class action lawsuit. Like mentioned before, minimum viable product.

In engineering terms, "hacking something together" would refer to taking a medley of various scraps and tidbits to create a useful tool or product that shouldn't be possible. When it comes to hacking, the idea is to overcome an obstacle or solve a problem using less effort and resources a human would need to make that obstacle or problem. Applied to any area in life, hacking becomes a performance-centered mindset—how can this be made to work right now?

There is no limit as to what can be used in hacking. Wherever the computer system is fortified with a human operator who is meant to double-check the system, a hacker can count on laziness or compliance.

Depending on sensors used in IoT devices, those with darker skin tones could find themselves unable to use them. In one instance[42], a bathroom soap dispenser installed at Facebook's headquarters couldn't recognize a black person waving his hand underneath it to drip soap but worked just fine when a white person did it. The workaround is to take a sheet of white paper towel and wave it underneath the sensor, after which it works as intended. This isn't an intentional design flaw but an omission on the part of the engineers who built the soap dispenser.

Dark skin absorbs more light while light skin reflects it, which confuses the sensor that measures the amount of light reflected into it. Engineers building the soap dispenser didn't test for enough of fringe cases because they were most likely urged to rush the product out as soon as possible and also keep its cost low; increasing the range of skin colors the soap dispenser detects would likely make it cost more and err more often. We are likely looking at a future filled with slick, fancy, overpriced IoT devices that work only in a narrow set of circumstances, but at least it is just a soap dispenser, right?

Sensors in self-driving cars could run the same fault as they fail to detect people with darker skin tones, thus smashing into them. One

---

42   https://www.youtube.com/watch?v=YJjv_OeiHmo

University of Georgia study analyzed by Metro.co.uk[43] found that self-driving cars tend to err 5% more when dark-skinned pedestrians were introduced in the test. Simply put, when engineers create a neural network to detect objects and pedestrians, they use the most glaringly obvious examples that help them create a working product in the least amount of time, which means white people because they stand out the most. Investors have shelled out money and want to see impressive results right now, but as mentioned previously, neural networks are probabilistic.

Vehicles currently require human drivers since no kind of software can react in a wide range of nuanced situations where a simple action or inaction can have fatal consequences, but at least we can assign blame to them. When a neural network in one such car finds itself in a completely novel situation, there is no telling what could happen with the Trolley Problem, a thought experiment in which a human has to make a split-second decision on whom to kill.

The Trolley Problem essentially asks if a human should divert a speeding trolley to kill one person instead of five or do nothing, letting five people die. A self-driving car might have to make the same kind of decision, but that one person would be the driver, and those five could be passers-by at a traffic light. When the self-driving car sees it can't avoid a potentially lethal collision with a group of people, it could opt to ram the nearest barrier, likely destroying itself and killing its driver. Coupled with the Chinese social credit score, we can easily imagine a dystopian future where citizens are ranked according to their value to the society at large and then suicided when someone of perceived higher value is in danger.

Hackers could simply wear blackface to reduce their chances of being seen by facial recognition software or detected by self-driving vehicles, becoming like ghosts or glitches ignored by the system.

---

43   https://metro.co.uk/2019/03/06/self-driving-cars-likely-run-black-people-8832676/

The real answer is that the acting human in a Trolley Problem situation should do whatever is necessary to save all the people, but nobody will blame him or her if they fail. Speeding trolleys would almost always be caused by a cascading failure of brakes and other safety mechanisms, which would necessitate investigation and revamp of those mechanisms—in short, a tragic event, such as that one would probably lead to better and stronger systems, not just a mechanical, binary decision to kill one or five people.

In 1988, a runaway train crashed into a stationary one at the French Gare de Lyon station, killing 56 people. As detailed in a Seconds from Disaster episode[44], the combination of passenger haste, design failures, and driver mistakes on a train where brakes could be easily disabled by accidentally leaning against the wrong handle led to the third worst peacetime rail accident in France. It is a tragedy that happens once a century and was ultimately caused by human mistake, but self-driving vehicles would aim to eliminate humans from the decision-making process altogether, potentially leading to this kind of event happening once a day without any recourse.

---

44   https://www.youtube.com/watch?v=HCM2aJAh2Jw

Chapter 23 – AI as Sports Referees

In sport, many things can be decided by a single centimeter, and a set of human referees might not be enough to get the right verdict in. With soccer, an ancient, brutal game derived from massive village brawls where an object was to be carried from one end of the field to the other, technology had to be introduced as humans kept finding ways to outsmart outdated rules. In one particularly painful instance in 1986, England lost to Argentina because one of the players, Diego Maradona, used his hand instead of his head to score a goal, which is a forbidden move. The incident came to be known as "Hand of God"[45] and was certainly what led to the adoption of high definition footage, a specialized video analysis team watching it that can call for a timeout and a set of high-speed cameras watching each goal.

As player performance increased, soccer was modernized by creating smaller, faster balls that could be kicked harder to create more impressive goals but that also meant the standard 24 frames per second TV cameras were not good enough for video analysis. Called Video Assistant Referee[46] (VAR), the setup provides several high-

---

45   https://www.youtube.com/watch?v=-ccNkksrfls

46   https://www.youtube.com/watch?v=pp431Y1Eqf0

speed camera angles to every inch of the field and lets the VAR team correct the on-field referee or just let them pause the game while they check the replay. Additionally, high-speed cameras watch each goal line to create a 3D representation of the ball as it is entering the goal to automatically signal to the referee through a bracelet screen and buzzer if a goal should be awarded. For just in case, there is a backup human referee with the sole purpose of staring at each goal line to double-check on VAR.

What VAR has shown us is that simply adding more humans to any given situation that calls for a judicious decision does not improve the accuracy, but simply adding more technology doesn't help either. The right solution is carefully scaling up the technology while adding backup humans because now we can afford it. The scare of "AI will leave truck drivers jobless" makes no sense if we can afford to hire a human driver, with people assisting AI and vice versa, just like in sport. Soccer is a now a sport where fame is made and lost based off of a single goal, so we better get it right every single time, with a damn good explanation if the system fails, which so far it hasn't done.

Could VAR decisions be challenged the same way we challenged pre-trial risk assessment scores? No, because VAR: a) shows all the raw data, meaning footage of the goal in close-up, high definition and slowed down and b) there's a human expert who examines the raw data and makes the call. Despite having ancient rules that resisted change for a long time, soccer was modernized when the audience, players, and referees easily adopted VAR because the system is transparent and redundant. Now that is the kind of AI technology we need, one that will be based on machines that work better than the human counterpart (cameras compared to the human eye) and readily challenged until we finally get it right, while still having the option of overriding the machine's decision.

Conclusion

Science fiction writers have been wringing their hands over artificial intelligence for decades, even before public figures ever discussed the concept. They imagined AI as a booster force that we will have to use to venture outside the solar system or just as an assistant that will help us fix things here on Earth, but an inescapable influence nonetheless. All the media that related the concept of AI to the general public slated it to be mysterious and analytical, doing whatever it takes to fulfill its own agenda before inevitably turning out to be the villain. As we have seen throughout this book, there is barely any evidence that will happen in this century.

What is happening is that entrepreneurs are pushing themselves harder than ever before to run their business ventures sleepless, fueled by stimulants, and frustrated by the lack of influence on politicians. So, when entrepreneurs do finally get some sleep, they have feverish dreams of an AI, a digital worker that could let them finally usurp the throne of political power and then take a nap. AI could even be presented as a deity to fill that missing hole in the lives of entire nations while giving it special legal privileges and immunities. Can tech giants actually do it? Highly doubtful.

The emergence of general AI, one as smart as a human being, is likely to require a technological invention as fundamental as electricity to function but one that humans won't be able to use because we will simply take the invention and again overperform compared to any machine. We do have a narrow AI, one that can compare images or find an object in a picture or recognize a certain face among a group of faces, but even that is worthless without a human handler overseeing it. Self-driving cars and trucks simply don't work without a human guardian and technician, meaning they are certain to increase employment rather than make people jobless.

As laid out throughout this book, general AI is merely a pipe dream, wishful thinking by tech giant CEOs who think their pet projects can be widely accepted and them hailed as saviors of humanity when they dole out UBI. None of the doom and gloom predictions they laid out are going to happen, but stoking fear does increase consumption and makes humans more malleable. So, now what? Just enjoy the ride.

Glossary

AI myths – Simplified ideas concerning AI spread through **clickbait**.

Attack surface – Probability a system or network will be successfully hacked. Exponentially increases with complexity.

Backdoor – Hidden access capability meant for spying and unauthorized access.

Big Data – Result of widespread automated collection and labeling of data points provided by humans using various software and hardware.

Clickbait – Content meant to entice a visit by the web user for the sole purpose of making ad revenue to the hosting website. Triggers the **limbic system**.

Cyberspace – Digital world. Rules of the physical, three-dimensional world need not apply there.

Deep learning – Smart computer program upgrading itself according to its own rules that we don't fully understand.

Defense in depth – Layering cheap, simple anti-hacking measures so that hackers give up in frustration.

Emergent property – Unplanned but useful property of a system.

Feature creep – Slowly increasing the scope of a software product, increasing its **attack surface** with a marginal increase in utility.

Free will – Ability to override actions of the **limbic system**.

General AI – Human-like AI. May become a lover or counselor.

Hacking – Human ingenuity in finding loopholes in computer systems.

Internet of things – Layer of robots that mediates between humans and the physical world.

Kernel – The core part of a computer. Imperturbable by users.

Limbic system – **Kernel** of the human brain. Obsessed with survival.

Machine learning – Any software that can change its output based on the data it's been fed.

Minimum viable product – Least amount of functionality a company can put into one product without getting sued for false advertising.

Narrow AI – Highly specialized AI, perhaps as smart as a mosquito.

Neural network – Layered **machine learning**, with the smart machine capable of organizing and upgrading itself.

Robotics – Giving a **neural network** a physical body with limited functionality.

SCS – See **Social credit system**.

Security by design – Minimizing **attack surface** by creating barebones services.

Singularity – Point where AI overtakes humans in all aspects, becoming **super AI**.

Social credit system – Chinese game-like scoring of citizens according to their value to the state to determine which are entitled to education and use of public transport.

Stress – Long-term breakdown of the body and psyche. Ultimate productivity booster.

Super AI – Godlike AI that will think in ways we can't comprehend.

Taboo – Sacred rule passed down through generations that mustn't be questioned or violated.

Turing complete – Originally used to mean a computer program that can fool humans into thinking it's a human too. It's nowadays taken as an inside joke since humans constantly evolve.

UBI – Universal basic income. It's touted as the universal answer to AI leaving people jobless.

UX – Programming paradigm that takes the user's **limbic system** into account.

VAR – Set of video analysis tools widely used in soccer since 2018 to detect illegal moves.

Here's another book by Neil Wilkins that you might like

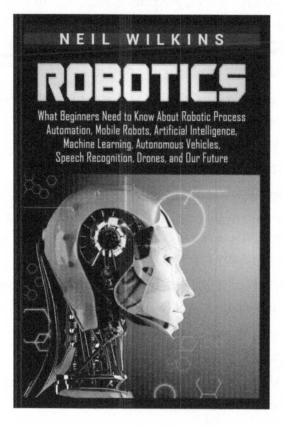

Made in the USA
Las Vegas, NV
17 October 2022

57520182R00069